MONOGRAPHS OF THE
SOCIETY FOR RESEARCH IN
CHILD DEVELOPMENT

Serial No. 261, Vol. 65, No. 2, 2000

ACROSS THE GREAT DIVIDE: BRIDGING THE GAP BETWEEN UNDERSTANDING OF TODDLERS' AND OLDER CHILDREN'S THINKING

Zhe Chen
Robert S. Siegler

WITH COMMENTARY BY
Marvin W. Daehler

MONOGRAPHS OF THE SOCIETY FOR RESEARCH IN CHILD DEVELOPMENT
Serial No. 261, Vol. 65, No. 2, 2000

CONTENTS

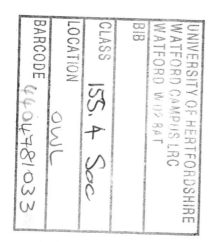

ABSTRACT

CHEN, ZHE, and ROBERT S. SIEGLER. Across the Great Divide: Bridging
the Gap Between Understanding of Toddlers' and Older Children's
Thinking. *Monographs of the Society for Research in Child Development*, 2000,
65(2, Serial No. 261).

Research on very young children's cognitive development differs greatly
from research on cognitive development in older children. The differences include the questions that are asked, the methods that are used to
address them, the measures that are employed to provide relevant evidence, and the level of detail at which children's knowledge is represented. The research approaches are so different that they create an
impression that infants' and toddlers' thinking differs qualitatively from
that of preschoolers and older children. This impression, however, may
reflect differences in research approaches rather than differences in children's thinking.

In the present study, we attempted to bridge this gap by applying to
toddlers a type of process analysis that has proved fruitful in studies of
older children. Overlapping waves theory, trial-by-trial strategy assessments, and microgenetic methods were used to analyze 1.5- and 2.5-year-
olds' problem solving and learning. The results demonstrated that changes
in toddlers' strategies could be assessed reliably on a trial-by-trial basis,
that the changes followed the basic form predicted by the overlapping
waves model, and that analyses of toddlers' strategies could tell us a great
deal about both qualitative and quantitative aspects of their learning.

A componential analysis of learning that previously had been applied
to older children also proved useful for understanding toddlers' learning.
The analysis specified that cognitive change frequently involves five components: acquisition of new strategies; strengthening of the strategies in
their original context; improved mapping of strategies onto novel problems; increasingly refined choices among variants of the strategies; and
increasingly skillful execution of the strategies. Independent measures
of these components indicated that strategic development in toddlers
involves improvements in all five components. Analyses of individual

differences in learning showed that the effects of distal variables, such as age and sex, could be partially explained in terms of their influence on mastery of the components, but that the distal variables exercised additional direct effects as well.

The process of learning in toddlers closely resembled that of older children in other ways as well. Like older children, toddlers use multiple strategies over the course of learning; their choices among strategies are quite adaptive from early on; their choices become progressively more adaptive as they gain experience with the task; they switch strategies not only from trial to trial but within a single trial; their transfer of learning from one problem to the next is primarily influenced by structural relations between problems but also is influenced by superficial features; they show utilization deficiencies early in learning that they gradually overcome; and they show individual differences in learning that fall into a few qualitatively distinct categories.

Perhaps most striking, the 1.5- and 2.5-year-olds emerged as active learners, who continued to work out the lessons of previous instruction in the absence of further instruction. That is, they integrated the lessons of their own problem-solving efforts with the previous instruction in ways that magnified the initial effects of the instruction. Overall, the findings indicated that the gap can be bridged; that theories, methods, measures, and representations of knowledge typically used with older children can improve our understanding of toddlers' problem solving and learning as well.

PREFACE

This *Monograph* examines change processes in toddlers' thinking. Although research on older children's cognitive development is focusing increasingly on this topic, little is known about how changes occur in the thinking of infants and toddlers. Even less is known about age-related differences in change processes within this period. Our goal in conducting the present study is to demonstrate that the type of process analysis that has proved highly informative in studying changes in older children's and adults' thinking can be equally informative in studying changes in the thinking of infants and toddlers.

In the sections below, we first describe the "great divide" that separates research on very early and later cognition. We next describe a current theoretical approach—the overlapping waves model—and a current methodology—the microgenetic method—that have been fruitfully applied to studying change processes in older children and adults. We argue that although this theory and method have not been applied to studying very young children's thinking, they should prove just as useful there as they have with older children. Then we describe the present study: what we did, what we found, and how the overlapping waves approach and microgenetic method allowed us to gain in-depth understanding of change processes in toddlers' problem solving.

I. THE GREAT DIVIDE

Current research on infants' and toddlers' thinking differs greatly from current research on the thinking of older children. The two bodies of research differ in the questions and issues that are emphasized, the experimental paradigms that are employed, the measures used to assess cognitive competence, and the level of detail at which thought processes are described. Some of these differences between the two bodies of research are due to inherent differences between younger and older children. Other reasons for the differences, however, are more historical and, from our perspective, unnecessary.

DIFFERENT QUESTIONS AND ISSUES

Most research on infant and toddler cognition has focused on establishing when particular competencies emerge. Among the competencies that have received extensive attention are imitation (Meltzoff, 1988), planning (Willatts, 1990), tool use (Brown, 1990), representing hidden objects (Baillargeon, 1987), forming expectations of future events (Haith, 1993), representing the number of objects (Wynn, 1998), and using external representations to find hidden objects (DeLoache, 1995). The basic theme that emerges from these and many other studies of infants' and toddlers' thinking can be summarized quite simply: Cognitive competencies are present, at least in rudimentary forms, at much younger ages than once suspected.

Research on infants and toddlers also has focused on developmental trends toward increasingly broad application of these early-emerging competencies. Such age-related improvements are evident in the range of causal relations that infants understand (Oakes, 1994), in the length of action sequences that they can plan (Willatts, 1990), in the set of physical symbols that toddlers can use to guide their searches for hidden objects (DeLoache, 1995), and in the rapidity with which they acquire problem-solving skills (Chen, Sanchez, & Campbell, 1997).

1

The issues that are most often addressed in current studies of older children's thinking overlap with those that are being addressed with infants and toddlers. For example, many studies of 4- to 8-year-olds focus on when they first show various competencies and on age-related improvements in the range of situations in which they exhibit these competencies. In the last decade, however, these types of research have been supplemented by an increasing number of studies aimed at revealing mechanisms of change in older children's thinking. The need to specify such mechanisms has long been recognized. For example, Flavell (1984) commented,

> Serious theorizing about basic mechanisms of cognitive growth has actually never been a popular pastime, now or in the past. It is rare indeed to encounter a substantive treatment of the problem in the annual flood of articles, chapters, and books on cognitive development. (p. 189)

Such implicit criticisms of the state of knowledge about change mechanisms, along with the inherent importance of the issue, have motivated a number of researchers who study preschoolers and older children to examine change processes empirically. These studies have already revealed quite a bit about change mechanisms, have the potential to reveal more, and have contributed to breaking down the once-rigid barrier between learning and development. In one reflection of this new focus, Kuhn (1995) commented,

> In the 1960s and 1970s, development was contrasted to a simplistic, nonrepresentational conception of learning that has little relevance today. Modern research has made it clear that learning processes share all of the complexity, organization, structure, and internal dynamics once attributed exclusively to development. If the distinction has become blurred, it is not because development has been reduced to "nothing but" learning, but rather because we now recognize learning to be more like development in many fundamental respects. (p. 138)

This increasing emphasis on change processes has been characterized as a "paradigm shift" in views of cognitive development (Granott, 1998).

One reason for the increasing emphasis on cognitive change processes is that studies that have focused on them have yielded clear commonalities regarding the basic properties of cognitive change. Consider just one of the consistent findings that has emerged—that discovery of new strategies is constrained by conceptual understanding (Coyle & Bjorklund, 1997; Gelman & Williams, 1998; Granott, 1993; Kuhn, Garcia-Mila, Zohar, & Andersen, 1995; Schauble, 1990, 1996). The novel strategies that children attempt generally make sense; they are not generated via blind trial and error. Newly generated strategies do not always yield correct solutions to the problems that elicited them, but they usually are reasonable efforts in that direction and usually conform to the basic principles that underlie legitimate strategies in the domain. This finding has been observed in such diverse areas as scientific reasoning, arithmetic, collaborative problem solving, memory strategies, and motor skills.

This and other consistent findings regarding the basic properties of cognitive change have motivated proposals regarding the mechanisms that result in these characteristics. One example comes from the domain of single-digit addition. To account for how children discover legitimate addition strategies without ever trying illegal ones, the idea of goal sketches has been proposed (Siegler & Jenkins, 1989), tested and supported through empirical experiments (Siegler & Crowley, 1994), and formally specified as a mechanism within a computer simulation of strategy discovery (Shrager & Siegler, 1998).

The same questions about change processes that are being addressed in studies of older children's thinking can be asked about younger children—and they are at least as interesting when applied to them. Consider one such question: Are the novel procedures attempted by infants and toddlers also constrained by conceptual understanding? No one knows. Only through direct observation of infants' and toddlers' construction of new procedures, and identification of the processes that give rise to the procedures, can such basic questions be answered.

DIFFERENT METHODS

As noted by Horowitz (1995) and by Haith and Benson (1998), the methods typically used to study infants' cognition differ considerably from those used to study preschoolers' and older children's cognition. Most research on infant cognition has employed looking-time paradigms, in particular habituation and preferential looking. Although these paradigms have the advantages of standardization and simplicity, several investigators have noted difficulties in interpreting the results that they yield (Haith & Benson, 1998; Russell, 1996). In particular, it often is difficult to specify the basis on which infants are discriminating among the displays. The paradigms also yield only the dichotomous outcome "discriminates/does not discriminate." Such depictions do not capture either the graded nature of most cognitive growth or the many small qualitative innovations that contribute so greatly to it.

Such concerns have led a number of investigators to begin using alternative paradigms that focus on infants' and toddlers' actions on objects. Procedures that examine reaching, sequential touching, and elicited imitation are among the most common alternatives to the looking paradigms

3

(Bauer & Mandler, 1992; Clifton, Muir, Ashmead, & Clarkson, 1993; Hofsten, Spelke, Feng, & Vishton, 1994; McCarty, Clifton, & Collard, 1999; Meltzoff & Moore, 1998; Willatts, 1998). Although experiments using such procedures constitute only a small minority of research on infants' and toddlers' cognition, they have extended knowledge in this area considerably. They have allowed examination of very young children's thinking in more natural contexts than those of the habituation paradigm and have yielded data that reflect the graded nature of early (and later) cognition.

To date, however, neither type of method has been used much to observe ongoing changes in infants' and toddlers' thinking. Much of the reason goes back to the questions that have been viewed as central in the area of early cognitive development. If the question of greatest interest is "What types of capabilities are present from early in development," standard cross-sectional methods are sufficient. If the central question, however, is "How do children acquire new knowledge," a different type of method is necessary. In particular, to provide maximally relevant data for addressing this question, it is essential to densely sample changing competence while the changes are occurring. Without such high-density sampling of changing competence, the specifics of the change process can only be the subject of speculation.

Microgenetic methods provide the type of high-density data needed to move beyond speculation regarding the change process. Such methods involve observing children's changing performance on a trial-by-trial basis during the period of rapid change (Kuhn, 1995; Siegler & Crowley, 1991). Studies using this approach have yielded the surprisingly consistent findings regarding cognitive change alluded to in the previous section (Kuhn, 1995; Miller & Coyle, 1999; Siegler, 1996).

Despite the usefulness of microgenetic methods for providing detailed information about cognitive change, such designs have not been used to examine infants' or toddlers' cognitive growth. Part of the problem is that certain means of assessing strategies on a trial-by-trial basis cannot be used with infants or toddlers. Verbal reports of strategy use provide one obvious example. Inability to use a particular measure, however, is not the same as inability to use a method; very young children's lack of articulateness simply means that alternative measures must be identified for assessing strategy use on each trial. One such means, a means that should prove applicable in many contexts, is illustrated in the present study.

DIFFERENT MEASURES

Research on infants' and toddlers' thinking, whether using looking-time paradigms or other approaches, has measured cognitive competence primarily in terms of the frequency of desired behaviors: imitating the model, reaching to the right location, showing renewed looking when a novel stimulus is shown or when a physically impossible event seems to occur, and so on. The questions that have been viewed as central have been crucial to this choice of measures, just as they have been crucial to choices of experimental paradigms. In particular, as discussed above, if the central question is "When can children do X," then evidence of above-chance levels of engaging in the desired behavior is highly informative. By contrast, if the central question is "How do children do X," or "Through what process of change do children become able to do X," then these measures tell only a small part of the story.

Research with older children and adults uses a considerably greater range of behavioral measures than does research on infants and toddlers. The additional measures include patterns of specific errors, solution-time patterns, eye movements, and verbal reports. Although infants and toddlers cannot generate very informative verbal reports, they can generate the other types of measures. Methods using such measures are frequently referred to as "process tracing methodologies," because they allow insights into the process through which the behavior was produced.

DIFFERENT REPRESENTATIONS OF KNOWLEDGE

The questions, methods, and measures used with older children have allowed their knowledge to be described in greater detail than current descriptions of infants' and toddlers' knowledge. Rather than simply indicating that the child "has" the relevant competence or capability, researchers who study older children often characterize their knowledge at the level of rules, strategies, and processing components that underlie their degree of success, the particular errors they make, and their pattern of solution times. Being able to assess children's knowledge at this relatively detailed level is crucial for examining change. Frequently, much of the increase in speed and accuracy that comes with age can be traced back to discovery of new rules and strategies (e.g., Amsel, Goodman, Savoie, & Clark, 1996; Brown & Burton, 1978; Siegler, 1987). Other times, the improved speed and accuracy reflect improved choices among alternative rules or strategies, rather than discovery of new approaches. Either way, detailed representation of children's knowledge is crucial for understanding the change process.

To summarize the arguments in this section, current research on infants' and toddlers' thinking differs from research on the thinking of older children in the questions that are being asked, the experimental methods and measures that are being used to answer them, and the level of detail at which knowledge is being represented. The gap is understandable, but it also is unfortunate. It creates artificial discontinuities in characterizations of cognitive development, artificial in the sense that they reflect changes in the way that investigators study children's thinking rather than changes in the thinking itself. One sign that the discontinuities are artificial comes in the paradoxical conclusions that emerge from the research. Research on the cognitive capabilities of infants and toddlers generally conveys an impression that they are highly cognitively competent. Research on the cognitive capabilities of preschoolers and school-age children often conveys an impression that they are cognitively incompetent. But are preschoolers and school-age children less cognitively competent than infants and toddlers? The problem is that the gap between the questions, methods, and measures used with infants and toddlers, on the one hand, and with older children, on the other, is so great that it becomes impossible to integrate the two literatures into a coherent depiction of cognitive development. The present study is an attempt to show that in addition to this gap being undesirable, it also is unnecessary. To this end, we describe recently developed theoretical and methodological approaches that are being applied to older children's thinking, and then describe how, in the present study, we applied these approaches to analyzing 1.5- and 2.5-year-olds' problem solving.

II. OVERLAPPING WAVES THEORY

Overlapping waves theory (Siegler, 1996) is based on three assumptions: (a) at any one time, children think in a variety of ways about most phenomena; (b) these varied ways of thinking compete with each other, not just during brief transition periods but rather over prolonged periods of time; and (c) cognitive development involves gradual changes in the frequency of these ways of thinking, as well as the introduction of more advanced ways of thinking.

Figure 1 provides a schematic illustration of these assumptions. Looking at any vertical slice of the figure indicates that multiple approaches are used at one time. Following the curve for any strategy indicates that strategies continue to be used for protracted periods. Looking horizontally across the figure indicates that the relative frequencies of all strategies shift gradually over time, with new strategies sometimes being added and older strategies sometimes ceasing to be used. Thus, the schematic

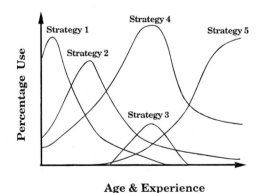

Age & Experience

FIGURE 1.—Schematic depiction of the overlapping waves model. NOTE. From *Emerging Minds: The Process of Change in Children's Thinking*, by Robert S. Siegler, 1996, Oxford: Oxford University Press. Copyright 1996 by Oxford University Press. Reprinted with permission.

7

diagram focuses attention on several key issues: the set of approaches (rather than the single approach) that children use at a given age, the factors that influence their choices among these approaches, the mechanisms that lead to changing frequencies of use of existing approaches, and the mechanisms that lead to discovery of new approaches.

Overlapping waves theory also postulates that the typical pattern of strategic development, shown in Figure 1, arises through the workings of five component processes: acquiring the strategy of interest, mapping the strategy onto novel problems, strengthening the strategy so that it is used consistently within given types of problems where it has begun to be used, refining choices among alternative strategies or alternative forms of a single strategy, and executing the strategy of interest increasingly effectively.

Acquiring new strategies is a necessary first step in strategic development; each strategy must begin to be used sometime. Such acquisition can occur through drawing analogies to better-understood problems, through forming mental models of the situation and reasoning about them, through observations made during the course of problem solving, or through direct verbal instruction (Anderson, 1991; Sternberg, 1985). Studies in which strategy use is classified on a trial-by-trial basis indicate that most children use three to six strategies to perform a given task (see Siegler, 1996, for a review of such studies). All of these strategies have to have been acquired at some point in development. Presenting children with novel tasks, or presenting them with large amounts of experience on somewhat familiar tasks, often allows observation of acquisition of new strategies (e.g., Siegler & Jenkins, 1989). Thus, the acquisition of new strategies is a fairly common event, one that is not limited to occasional transition periods and one that can be studied directly.

Mapping the strategy onto novel problems becomes essential once a strategy is acquired. Strategy acquisition inevitably takes place in a particular context. Generalizing the strategy from that context to other contexts in which the strategy is applicable can be a formidable task. The challenge is similar to that faced in vocabulary acquisition (Anglin, 1993), where the learner must be able to extend the new word to all cases in which it is applicable and to avoid extending it to cases in which it is inapplicable. As with vocabulary acquisition, successful mapping of new strategies to novel situations requires the problem solver to distinguish relevant from irrelevant aspects of the situation in which the new cognitive entity was initially acquired. Mapping the strategy to new problems on the basis of similarity between superficial features of the original and novel situations leads to the strategy being used where it is not applicable, to it not being used where it is applicable, or both. In contrast, understanding the principles that govern applicability of the strategy results in appropriate mapping of the new approach.

Strengthening the newly acquired strategy, both in the original context and in the contexts to which it is mapped, is a third component of learning. Given that children use multiple ways of thinking over prolonged periods of time, and given that some of the ways of thinking are more advanced than others, the quality of children's thinking can improve if they increase their reliance on new, relatively advanced approaches and decrease their reliance on older, less advanced ones. Such strengthening of relatively sophisticated approaches within the existing set of approaches is a more common vehicle of cognitive growth than is commonly recognized. Both children and adults frequently fail to rely on new strategies that they have acquired, even when those strategies are considerably more effective than older alternatives (Acredolo, O'Conner, & Horobin, 1989; Church & Goldin-Meadow, 1986; Siegler, 1995). Difficulties in retrieving the new strategy and difficulties in inhibiting older strategies are likely causes of the limited use of new approaches.

Refining choices among alternative versions of a strategy is the fourth key learning component. Even if both the set of strategies and the overall frequency of each strategy remain constant, use of each strategy can be concentrated increasingly on those problems on which the strategy is most useful. This is not just a logical possibility. Although preschoolers' and older children's strategy choices tend to be adaptive from early in learning, the degree of adaptiveness often increases as they gain experience in the domain (Karmiloff-Smith, 1979; Lemaire & Siegler, 1995). For example, Lemaire and Siegler (1995) found that over the course of a year, French second graders who were learning single-digit multiplication increasingly often chose the strategy that yielded the most efficient performance on the particular type of problem.

Increasingly effective execution of new strategies is the fifth and final component within this analysis of learning. Even if there are no changes in the set of strategies that have been acquired, in the breadth of problems onto which each strategy is mapped, in the frequency of each strategy on both original and transfer problems, and in the precision of choices among the strategies, children's accuracy and speed can improve greatly as they gain practice in executing each approach. In the Lemaire and Siegler (1995) study, for example, on those problems on which children retrieved answers to a given multiplication problem at all three times of measurement, percentage of errors decreased from 23% to 2%, and mean solution time decreased from 4 s to 2 s. Utilization deficiencies, in which use of a new strategy does not lead to enhanced performance until their execution of the strategy improves, also illustrate the importance of this source of development (Coyle & Bjorklund, 1997; Miller & Seier, 1994).

These five components of strategic change—acquiring, mapping, strengthening, refining, and executing—are illustrated in Figure 2, in rough

9

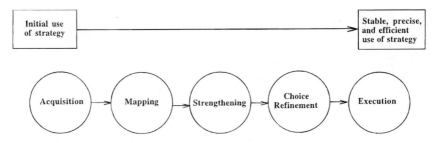

FIGURE 2.—Five components of strategic change, in rough sequential order.

sequential order. The sequence is roughly sequential, rather than precisely so, because learning of the components overlaps, rather than one process being mastered before learning of the next begins. For example, mapping a strategy from the original context in which it was learned to a new problem overlaps with strengthening the strategy so that it is used more often. Figure 2 does, however, provide a rough sense of the learning sequence, in that children must acquire a strategy in an initial context before mapping it to different problems, must know several strategies before refining their choices among them, and so on.

Data consistent with the overlapping waves model have been obtained across such varied tasks as serial recall, tic-tac-toe, arithmetic, time telling, spelling, reading, locomotor activity, rule learning, moral reasoning, and scientific experimentation (Adolph, 1997; Crowley & Siegler, 1999; Goldin-Meadow, Alibali, & Church, 1993; Granott, 1993; Karmiloff-Smith, 1979; Kuhn, Garcia-Mila, Zohar, & Andersen, 1995; McGilly & Siegler, 1990; Rittle-Johnson & Siegler, 1999; Schauble, 1990, 1996; Siegler, 1988; Siegler & McGilly, 1989; Thelen & Ulrich, 1991; Turiel & Davidson, 1986). In all of these areas, children have been found to use multiple strategies at any given age, with the variability existing within individual children as well as between children. In each area, children have been found to shift toward more advanced approaches with age and experience. The components summarized above also have been found to play important roles in preschoolers' and older children's learning of a wide variety of tasks (Lemaire & Siegler, 1995; Siegler, 1995; Siegler & Chen, 1998; Siegler & Stern, 1998).

Moreover, computational models of strategy choice and strategy discovery have been formulated that generate patterns of change that closely resemble both the overlapping waves formulation and empirical data on children's performance (Shrager & Siegler, 1998; Siegler & Shipley, 1995). These simulation models suggest that the overlapping waves pattern arises through a mix of strategy discovery and strategy choice processes. More

10

specifically, the system's problem-solving experience generates an increasingly extensive database regarding the properties of both strategies and problems. This database, together with the system's basic architecture, makes possible discovery of new strategies, increased reliance on relatively advanced preexisting strategies, mapping of strategies onto novel problems, increasingly refined choices among strategies, and increasingly fast and accurate execution of strategies.

Overlapping waves theory also suggests a new agenda for studies of infants' and toddlers' cognition. Rather than trying to identify *the* age at which children develop a given competence or capability, we would trace over time the set of approaches that they use, paying attention to changing distributions of existing approaches as well as to the emergence of new approaches. We also would examine how emergence of a new approach changes choices among previous approaches. For example, we would try to learn whether use of the new approach comes completely at the expense of the least advanced existing approach, whether it comes proportionately from all of the existing approaches, or whether it comes primarily at the expense of the most advanced of the existing approaches (as would happen if both the new approach and the most advanced previous approach were used primarily on the most challenging problems in the domain). Finally, we would examine the circumstances surrounding discovery of new approaches. All of these goals can be addressed through the use of microgenetic methods.

III. MICROGENETIC METHODS

Obtaining a precise understanding of cognitive change requires observing such changes while they are occurring. Traditional cross-sectional and longitudinal designs do not allow precise analyses of change, because the observations of intellectual competence are separated too far in time for much to be learned about the change process. This wide spacing of observations leaves open a large number of possible pathways to change. The problem is especially great because changes in children's thinking often do not proceed by the most direct route imaginable. After discovering more advanced new approaches, children often temporarily abandon the new ways of thinking and regress to less sophisticated ones. This is true even when the children have stated compelling explanations for why the new approach is superior (Siegler & Jenkins, 1989). Exacerbating the problem, individual children often vary in their paths of change (e.g., Karmiloff-Smith, 1984; Piaget, 1971). A strategy that is transitional to a more advanced approach for some children may not be used at all by others (Kuhn et al., 1995; Schauble, 1996; Siegler & Stern, 1998).

Microgenetic methods offer a promising way to meet the challenges inherent in trying to understand change processes. The approach is defined by three characteristics: (a) an observation period spanning the time from the beginning of the period of rapid change to the stable use of target ways of thinking; (b) a high density of observations during this period, relative to the rate of change; and (c) intensive, trial-by-trial assessments of ongoing changes, both qualitative and quantitative. For recent perspectives on microgenetic methods and what they have taught us, see Kuhn (1995) and Miller and Coyle (1999).

A study conducted by Schauble (1996) illustrates how microgenetic methods can yield information about change that could not be attained using traditional cross-sectional or longitudinal designs. Fifth graders and adults were asked repeatedly over six sessions to generate experiments that would indicate the causal roles of each of four variables. Both the children and the adults increased their understanding of the impact of

12

the variables through their experiments. The progress, however, was far from direct. Cases of learning rarely involved children or adults progressing from an incorrect understanding of a variable to a correct understanding and then maintaining that correct understanding. Instead, more than 80% of belief revisions involved at least three changes back and forth, and some involved as many as eight. Both adults and 11-year-olds frequently returned to incorrect beliefs that they had earlier explicitly rejected on the basis of contrary evidence, though adults did so somewhat less often. Without the trial-by-trial analyses afforded by the microgenetic method, such regressions and jagged paths of change would not have been detected.

Microgenetic methods have proved useful for studying a wide range of age groups, content domains, and issues. They have been used to study cognitive change in preschoolers (e.g., Siegler & Jenkins, 1989), school-age children (e.g., Coyle & Bjorklund, 1997), adolescents and college students (Kuhn et al., 1995), and elderly adults (Siegler & Lemaire, 1997). They have been used to study change in domains as diverse as attention (Miller & Aloise-Young, 1996), memory (Bjorklund, Coyle, & Gaultney, 1992), arithmetic computation (Siegler & Jenkins, 1989), mathematical principles (Alibali & Goldin-Meadow, 1993), conceptual understanding (Metz, 1998), social problem solving (Wertsch & Hickmann, 1987), scientific reasoning (Kuhn et al., 1995; Schauble, 1996), pictorial representation (Karmiloff-Smith, 1986, 1992), and analogical reasoning (Chen & Klahr, 1999). Among the issues that they have allowed researchers to study are developmental differences in learning (Coyle & Bjorklund, 1997; Kuhn et al., 1995; Metz, 1998; Schauble, 1996) and the relation between initial knowledge and the acquisition of new knowledge (Alibali, 1999; Staszewski, 1988).

Microgenetic methods have proven particularly useful for studying individual differences. The reason is the large amount of data they yield about each child's learning. They allow us to identify differences in the types of strategies that children use initially, in the benefits they derive from various types of experiences, and in the path of change that their thinking follows.

Microgenetic studies also have suggested a useful conceptual distinction for thinking about individual differences in cognitive change. The distinction is between distal and proximal influences on change (Siegler & Chen, 1998). Distal influences are characteristics that children bring with them to the experiment: age, sex, IQ, content knowledge, and so on. Proximal influences are processes that children execute in the course of the experiment, such as the five components in Figure 2. Many analyses of individual differences in older children and adults have linked variation in distal variables to variation in learning outcomes. For example,

13

older children, children with higher IQs, and children with greater initial knowledge all tend to learn more from relevant experience (Coyle & Bjorklund, 1997; Johnson & Mervis, 1994; Schneider, Korkel, & Weinert, 1989). These distal influences, however, presumably exercise their influence by affecting the proximal processes that occur during the course of the experiment. For example, children with greater initial content knowledge may learn more quickly and completely because they more accurately encode stimulus displays, better recall information from prior trials, generate higher quality analogies to comparable past situations, and so on. These proximal processes directly produce learning in the experimental situation. In microgenetic studies with older children, successful execution of proximal processes that occur earlier in the learning sequence has been found to exercise large influences on success in executing subsequent processes (Rittle-Johnson, 1999; Siegler & Chen, 1998). Usually, the immediately preceding proximal component exerts the largest influence. Distal influences, however, can and fairly often do exert an additional influence, above and beyond that of the proximal processes.

Microgenetic methods have been adopted by researchers with a variety of theoretical perspectives: Piagetian (Inhelder et al., 1976), Vygotskian (Wertsch & Hickmann, 1987), dynamical systems (Thelen & Ulrich, 1991), and information processing (Bjorklund & Coyle, 1995). Despite the investigators' varying theoretical predispositions and the diverse content domains to which microgenetic methods have been applied, the descriptions of change that have emerged from the studies are strikingly similar. One consistent finding was cited earlier—that discovery of new strategies is conceptually constrained. Another consistent finding is that cognitive change tends to be gradual. Older, less powerful ways of thinking about a task usually continue to be employed for a long time after newer, more advanced ways of thinking about it are also available (Kuhn, 1995; Metz, 1985; Schauble, 1990, 1996; Siegler, 1994). A third consistent phenomenon that has emerged from microgenetic studies is that discoveries are made when children have been succeeding on the task as well as when they have been failing (Karmiloff-Smith, 1992; Miller & Aloise-Young, 1996; Siegler & Jenkins, 1989). Necessity can be the mother of invention, but new ideas also emerge without any external pressure. Yet a fourth consistent finding is consistent positive relations between the initial variability of thinking and the subsequent rate of learning. In many, but not all studies, the greater the initial variability, the more likely that children will generate useful new problem-solving strategies (Alibali & Goldin-Meadow, 1993; Goldin-Meadow, Alibali, & Church, 1993; Graham & Perry, 1993; Siegler, 1995).

These consistent phenomena, in turn, have given rise to a set of intriguing proposals regarding the processes that produce the changes. To account for the persistent use of nonoptimal strategies, despite more effective strategies being known, the construct of utilization deficiency has been proposed (Bjorklund & Coyle, 1995; Miller & Seier, 1994). To account for why discoveries occur when existing strategies are producing successful performance, the SCADS computer simulation progressively frees cognitive resources as it gains experience executing existing strategies, thus making possible construction of effective new strategies (Shrager & Siegler, 1998). To account for positive relations between initial variability and subsequent learning, investigators have focused on the ways in which variable behavior reveals the possibilities inherent in the task environment, which often leads to discovery of useful new approaches (Neuringer, 1993; Stokes, 1995).

Although microgenetic approaches have become an increasingly important approach in examining older children's cognition, they rarely have been used to study infants' or toddlers' thinking. Perhaps the most important reason was alluded to earlier: The questions that have been dominant in the area have given little incentive to those studying infants' and toddlers' thinking to use microgenetic methods. A second important reason involves the logistics of doing research with infants and toddlers. Children of these ages have relatively short attention spans and lack the verbal facility to explain their reasoning. Studying their thinking microgenetically would require relatively short sessions and use of nonverbal methods to assess strategy use.

Fortunately, these considerations in no way preclude use of microgenetic techniques with infants and toddlers. Although such young children cannot generate verbal reports, they do generate a great deal of overt behavior that can be at least as useful for inferring strategy use on a trial-by-trial basis. With well-chosen tasks and age groups, trial-by-trial analyses can reveal a considerable amount of change within a relatively short session or series of sessions. Most important, the inherent importance of change in the lives of infants and toddlers means that we must understand it better if we are ever to have a comprehensive understanding of children's thinking. Indeed, the omnipresence and rapidity of change during the first years of life suggest that using microgenetic methods to study very young children could lead to especially great advances in understanding.

One of the very few microgenetic studies of infants illustrates the type of advances that this method can yield. The study (Adolph, 1997) examined how infants and toddlers learn to locomote up and down ramps of varying slopes. Adolph followed the infants at frequent intervals from the time when crawling was their predominant mode of locomotion on flat surfaces to the time when walking had become dominant. The research indicated that the infants and toddlers used a variety of strategies for going up and down the ramps: crawling, walking, sliding on their

15

bellies, sliding on their behinds, and so on. Adolph also found that the infants and toddlers adjusted their locomotor strategies to the demands of the tasks. They used their predominant mode of locomotion on relatively shallow slopes, but when they needed to descend down steeper slopes, they relied more often on safer strategies, such as sliding down feet first. She also found that the precision of infants' choices reached quite high levels by the end of the period in which crawling was their predominant mode of locomotion, but that it regressed substantially when walking became their predominant mode. Although Adolph conceptualized her findings within a motor development framework, the study also suggests that microgenetic methods can be used to study infants' and toddlers' acquisition of problem-solving skills.

IV. THE PRESENT STUDY

THE TASK

In the study described in this *Monograph*, we applied a microgenetic method to examine 1.5- and 2.5-year-olds' acquisition of a problem-solving skill. The task that we examined required the toddlers to use simple tools, such as a toy rake or a toy cane, to pull in a toy that was too distant for them to reach. Toddlers' tool use was of interest because ability to use tools to solve problems is a classic measure of intelligence in both people and nonhuman primates (Goodall, 1986; Kohler, 1925; Visalberghi & Limongelli, 1994); because such tool use requires understanding causal relations, a key part of early cognitive development (Keil, 1989; Leslie, 1982; Oakes & Cohen, 1995); and because efforts to solve the task generate a great deal of visible behavior from which strategy use can be inferred. The task also presents a particularly clear demand for means-end reasoning. This is a central problem-solving skill, which involves comparing the current situation to a goal and progressively reducing the differences between them until the goal is met. Such reasoning underlies problem solving in a great many situations from infancy (Willatts, 1984; Willatts & Rosie, 1989) to adulthood (Newell & Simon, 1972).

The tool-use task that we presented was similar to one described by Brown (1990). Children were presented an attractive toy that was on a table in front of them but that was out of reach. On the table between the child and the toy were six potential tools that might be used to retrieve the toy. Only one of the tools was both long enough and had the right kind of head to be effective for this purpose. Depending on the problem, this target tool could be a toy rake, cane, or ladle. The other tools were either too short to reach the toy, had the wrong kind of head for pulling (e.g., an oar), or had no head (i.e., a straight stick).

As illustrated in Table 1, the task involved a series of three problems. On the first three trials of the first problem (Problem A), children in all three conditions were encouraged to obtain the toy and were told they

17

TABLE 1

Design of Experiment

	Trial					
	Pretraining				Posttraining	
Problem	1	2	3		4	5
A				Modeling,		
B				hint, or no		
C				instruction	—	—

Note.—Posttraining problems were not included on Problem C.

could use the tools to do so, but were given no more specific instruction. These pretraining trials provided a measure of the toddlers' baseline performance. Then, children in the modeling condition saw the experimenter demonstrate how to use the target tool to obtain the toy, children in the hint condition heard the experimenter encourage them to use the target tool to obtain the toy, and children in the control condition were not given any instruction. Following this, children in all conditions were presented two posttraining trials on that problem, to determine if children in the modeling and hint conditions had learned from the instruction. After completing Problem A, children in all three conditions were presented Problem B, which differed from Problem A in the particular tools and toy, and in some other superficial ways, but on which the same strategy would be effective. Again, children in all conditions were given three trials prior to training, then those in the modeling and hint conditions received the modeling or the hint, respectively, and then, children in all three conditions were presented two posttraining trials. Finally, children in all three groups were presented Problem C, which differed from Problems A and B in the particulars of the toy and tools and in other superficial aspects, but on which the same strategy would work again.

Brown (1990) found that on a similar task, 2- and 3-year-olds who were trained to use the most effective tool could transfer their learning to a superficially dissimilar problem. For example, when children who had been trained to use a rake with a red-and-white striped pattern were presented a transfer problem, they usually chose the functionally similar toy (e.g., a solid red cane) rather than a straight stick with the red-and-white pattern or the head of a rake. This finding established the age-appropriateness of the task for examining toddlers' problem solving.

In addition to being age-appropriate, the toy-retrieval task had several major advantages for conducting a microgenetic study. One was that young children find it interesting. Microgenetic studies require repeated trials so that changes in children's thinking can be examined. Such repetition makes it essential to select a task that motivates children and attracts their attention, at least to the extent that they continue to try hard over repeated trials.

Another major advantage of the toy-retrieval task for conducting a microgenetic study of young children's learning was that it allowed straightforward assessment of their strategy on each trial. We could see whether the children's strategy was to (a) lean forward and reach for the toy with their hand, (b) turn to their parent and ask for help, (c) use one of the tools to reach for the toy, or (d) just sit and look at the toy or engage in some other activity not directed at obtaining the toy, such as waving a tool in the air. Of course, they could, and sometimes did, engage in several of these strategies on a given trial. We also could assess their strategy use at the more specific level of which of the tools they chose on each trial in which they used some tool. For these reasons, toddlers' lack of articulateness was no problem in assessing their strategy use on this task; their overt behavior provided incontrovertible evidence of which strategy they used.

A third advantage of the toy-retrieval task was that it was easy to create multiple structurally parallel problems. The problems shared the same goal structure and allowed the same type of solution. They differed, however, in the toy that was being retrieved, in the color and patterns of the target tool and of the other five tools, and in the exact form of the target tool (rake, cane, or ladle). These isomorphic forms of the problem allowed us to assess not only learning in the context of the original problem but also transfer of the learned skills to new problems with different tools and toy. Together, the multiple problems and the multiple trials on each problem allowed us to examine whether toddlers relied primarily on superficial or structural similarities among tools in choosing which tool to use on new problems.

A fourth advantageous feature of the toy-retrieval task was that it allowed us to examine children's ability to learn from their own problem-solving experience. As shown in Table 1, all children received three trials on each problem before any instruction was given on that problem. Children's ability to transfer to Problem B what they learned from instruction on Problem A should be evident on the first trial of Problem B. If toddlers can learn from their own problem-solving experience, however, their performance should improve over the first three trials of Problem B, despite their not receiving any instruction in this period. Instruction does more than convey specific information, such as that a particular tool is the one to use to get a toy. It also can create a structure for interpreting subsequent experience. Having such a structure may allow children to learn lessons from their experience that the same experience would not have conveyed without the prior instruction. If this view of instruction is correct, then children in the modeling and hint conditions should show greater gains over the pretraining trials within Problems B and C than children in the control condition.

Thus, the toy-retrieval task had much to recommend it for a microgenetic study of toddlers' acquisition of a problem-solving skill. It was within their problem-solving capabilities, was sufficiently interesting that they would remain motivated over repeated trials, elicited unambiguous overt behavior so that strategy use could be assessed reliably on each trial, allowed assessment of transfer as well as initial learning, and allowed assessment of strategic variability within each problem as well as general trends across problems.

STRATEGIES FOR PERFORMING THE TASK

What means might toddlers use to obtain the toy? The one strategy that could lead to success in the experimental context was using a tool (the *tool strategy*). Children, however, could also try at least three other approaches. They could lean forward and reach for the toy (the *forward strategy*), they could ask their parent for help (the *indirect strategy*), or they could just sit facing the toy and hope that it was given to them *(no strategy)*. In the toddlers' past experience, all three of these strategies seem likely to have led to attaining goals more often than the tool strategy. Infants and toddlers frequently obtain desired objects by leaning forward and reaching for them (e.g., Clifton, Muir, Ashmead, & Clarkson, 1993), they often use their parents as tools for obtaining toys that are out of reach (Mosier & Rogoff, 1994), and informal observation indicates that parents and siblings frequently give babies toys that the baby is looking at. In contrast, using physical objects to retrieve toys seems likely to be a novel activity for infants and toddlers. Consistent with this analysis, for the first few trials of the present study, toddlers used all three of the alternative approaches more often than they used the tool strategy.

As is often the case, strategy choice on the toy-retrieval task involved a hierarchical set of choices. Toddlers needed to choose not only among the four strategies listed in the last paragraph; those who chose the tool strategy needed to make the further choice of which tool to use. Children could choose the target tool, but they also could choose tools that were deficient in one or more ways. Thus, children needed to learn both to choose a tool and to choose the right tool.

LEARNING CONDITIONS

As briefly described above, children participated in one of three learning conditions: modeling, hint, or control. We chose to examine the effects of modeling and verbal hints on toddlers' learning because showing and telling toddlers how to solve problems are common practices in the everyday environment and because it seemed likely that they would be effective in the current situation. There was good reason to think that toddlers could benefit from the modeling procedure, both in terms of learning to solve the original problem and in terms of transferring the learning to new problems. Even before their first birthday, children can learn to achieve goals by imitating novel sequences of actions modeled by an adult (e.g., Bauer & Mandler, 1992; Case, 1985; Meltzoff, 1988). Toddlers just beyond their first birthday also have been shown able to generalize imitated actions to novel materials when some of the original props are replaced by new ones (Barnat, Klein, & Meltzoff, 1996; Bauer & Dow, 1994; Chen, Sanchez, & Campbell, 1997). Such imitation and generalization of action sequences provides infants with a powerful learning tool, one that makes possible the acquisition of problem-solving strategies that they see other people use.

Although very young children can imitate modeled behaviors and can transfer them to somewhat different situations, the consistency and rapidity with which they do so improves considerably with age and experience. In all of the above-cited studies that compared older and younger children, the older children learned more completely and more quickly. Thus, developmental differences in learning seem to be omnipresent at this early age, as they are later in development.

These developmental differences notwithstanding, past studies have demonstrated that infants and toddlers should be able to learn to solve toy-retrieval problems. Demonstrating that infants and toddlers can learn a skill, however, is not the same as specifying how they learn it. The componential analysis described in the next section was generated with this goal in mind.

APPLYING OVERLAPPING WAVES THEORY TO THE TOY RETRIEVAL TASK

As noted earlier, overlapping waves theory postulates that acquisition of new strategies involves five learning components. The componential analysis seemed as applicable to toddlers' learning of the toy retrieval task as to older children's learning of more complex problems.

In the toy-retrieval context, the first component, acquisition of the new strategy, involves beginning to use tools to reach for the toy. Although using a tool to get the toy would strike adults and older children as obviously the best approach, for toddlers the competing approaches of learning forward to reach for the toy or asking parents for help seemed likely to be strong competitors. Young children seemed likely to have past

21

histories of obtaining desired objects through those means but not through using tools. Without modeling or hints, it was unclear whether most toddlers would use a tool anytime during the session.

The second component involved mapping the tool strategy from the problem on which it was first used onto subsequent, superficially different, problems. Again, this seemed likely to present a challenge for toddlers. A number of contextual factors varied from each problem to the next: the identity of the toy that children were trying to obtain, the color and material of the table on which the toy was placed, whether the children were sitting or standing, and so on. In addition, the tool that had allowed children to obtain the toy in one problem was never present in later ones. Children had to map the tool strategy from the previous problem to the new one, despite these differences between the problems.

The third learning component in the toy retrieval context involved strengthening the tool strategy. Using a tool on a given trial did not guarantee its continued use. Based on previous observations of older children's strategy use, strengthening seemed likely to occur gradually over problems and over trials within a single problem.

The fourth component, strategy refinement, needed to be made at several hierarchically related levels. As shown in Figure 3, children needed to choose the tool strategy, rather than leaning forward or asking their parent's help, and they also needed to choose the target tool, rather than one of the five alternative tools. The tools that were presented on the three problems were constructed so that if children chose tools on new problems by trying to match perceptually compelling superficial features of the previous target tool, they would fail to obtain the toy. For example, if on Problem A, the target tool had red vertical stripes, then on Problem B, two ineffective tools would have red vertical stripes and the target tool would not. If toddlers understood the causal properties that led to previ-

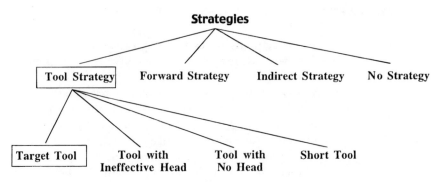

FIGURE 3.—The hierarchy of strategies among which children needed to choose.

ous target tools being effective in obtaining the toy, they presumably would prefer the new target tool to alternatives that were more perceptually similar to previous ones. By contrast, if their understanding of the modeling or verbal hint was not conceptually constrained in this way, they would be slow to distinguish essential from incidental properties of previous target tools and to consistently choose the new target tool.

The final learning component involves strategy execution. Even if children chose the target tool, they still might fail to obtain the toy. A certain amount of skill in using the cane, rake, or ladle was necessary for the right choice to yield the desired goal.

Thus, we expected toddlers' learning to incorporate the same five component processes as older children's and adults' acquisition of problem-solving skills that are equally novel to them. Using the same components, however, in no way precluded age-related differences in children's learning. To the contrary, such age-related differences were expected to be present in the effectiveness with which older and younger children executed all five processes. Development was expected to occur not in which processes were components of learning but in the likelihood of successful implementation of each component.

GOALS OF THE PRESENT RESEARCH

In the present study, we pursued three types of goals: specific, intermediate, and high-level. The specific goal was to understand how toddlers learn to use tools to solve problems. Tool use is one of the basic characteristics that distinguishes human beings and, to a lesser extent, a few other types of primates from other animals. The findings of Brown (1990) indicate that toddlers are capable of using tools to meet their goals. The present study was designed to reveal the learning processes through which they become able to do so.

An intermediate goal of the study was to test the usefulness of the componential analysis of learning and transfer with a much younger population than heretofore examined. Similar componential analyses have proved useful for analyzing preschool and elementary school-age children's acquisition of competence in arithmetic (Lemaire & Siegler, 1995), number conservation (Siegler, 1995), and scientific reasoning (Siegler & Chen, 1998). Determining which components cause the most difficulty, and whether the relative difficulty differs for older and younger children, seems likely to be useful for characterizing learning on a range of tasks. The componential analysis also provides a common framework for comparing the learning of infants and toddlers with that of preschoolers, elementary school children, adolescents, and adults.

Our most general goal was to demonstrate the usefulness of overlapping waves theory and microgenetic methods for studying very young children. Almost all past studies in which this theory and methodology have been applied have utilized older children. This is not coincidental. Immediately retrospective verbal reports provide a convenient and widely useful means for assessing strategy use on a trial-by-trial basis. Solution times, which often provide converging evidence for the verbal reports, are also more easily interpretable with older children and adults. The reason is that chronometric methods presuppose participants who are trying to answer as quickly as possible, something that is difficult to assume with infants or toddlers. Thus, it is not surprising that most evidence for strategic variability, most microgenetic studies, and most applications of overlapping waves theory have involved older children. The potential usefulness of this theory and methodology, however, are as great with very young children as with older ones. Indeed, given the omnipresence of learning in the lives of infants and toddlers, and the frequency with which their thinking is reflected in their overt behavior, the theory and methodology may prove to be especially useful for studying them. Thus, the most general goal of this study was to demonstrate the types of insights into change processes that can be gained by applying the overlapping waves theory, componential framework, and microgenetic methods to very young children.

V. METHOD

PARTICIPANTS

Eighty-six toddlers between 18 and 35 months of age participated in the study. The toddlers were divided into a younger group of forty-two 18- to 26-month-olds and an older group of forty-four 27- to 35-month-olds. Children were randomly assigned to one of three experimental conditions, thus creating six groups: modeling-young (N = 16; mean age = 21.6 months); modeling-old (N = 15; mean age = 30.2 months); hint-young (N = 16; mean age = 21.8 months); hint-old (N = 12; mean age = 30.4 months); control-young (N = 12; mean age = 22.2 months); and control-old (N = 15; mean age = 30.5 months). Approximately the same proportion of boys and girls were assigned to each condition. An additional 9 children were tested, but their data were not included in the analyses, due to their crying or becoming unhappy during the procedure and therefore not being able to complete it. The experimenters were a female research assistant in her 20s and a male postdoctoral fellow in his 30s.

TASK AND MATERIALS

As shown in Figure 4, children started each problem facing a table, either standing or sitting on their parent's lap. An attractive toy was in the middle of the table, too far away for the child to reach (children were not allowed to climb on the table). In one problem, the toy was a turtle; in another, a bird; and in the third, an Ernie doll. Each toy generated a distinctive sound.

On the table, between the child and the toy, were six potential tools (Figure 5). Only one of them—the *target tool*—was likely to be useful for obtaining the toy, because it was the only one that had a long enough shaft and a head at a right angle to the shaft so that it could be used to pull the toy to the child. The other tools were less useful than the target

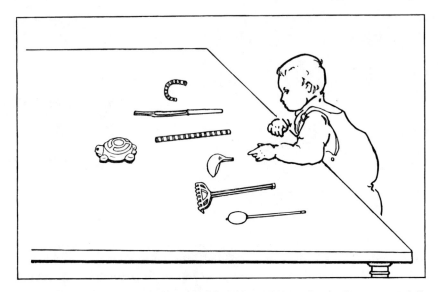

FIGURE 4.—The toy-retrieval task. The child needed to choose the target tool (in this illustration, the toy rake) to pull in the toy (in this case, the turtle).

tool because they were too short, had no head, or had an ineffective head (e.g., a tool shaped like an oar). On each problem, the six tools included one with an ineffective head, two with no head, two with shafts too short to reach the toy, and the target tool. Each of the four long tools was about 14 in. long; the short tools were 5–6 in.

As shown in Figure 5, the target tools on successive problems differed along several dimensions, including the color and pattern of the shaft and the shape of the head at the end of the tool (rake, cane, or ladle). All target tools, however, enabled children to achieve the same function— pulling in the toy—in essentially the same way. The six tools on Problem B were related to the target tool on Problem A as follows:

> *Target tool*: Same length shaft, functionally similar but different-shaped head, different color and pattern;

> *Ineffective head tool*: Same length shaft, functionally dissimilar and different-shaped head, different color and pattern;

> *No head tool 1*: Same length shaft, no head, same color and pattern;

> *No head tool 2*: Same length shaft, no head, different color and pattern;

Problem   Tools and Toy

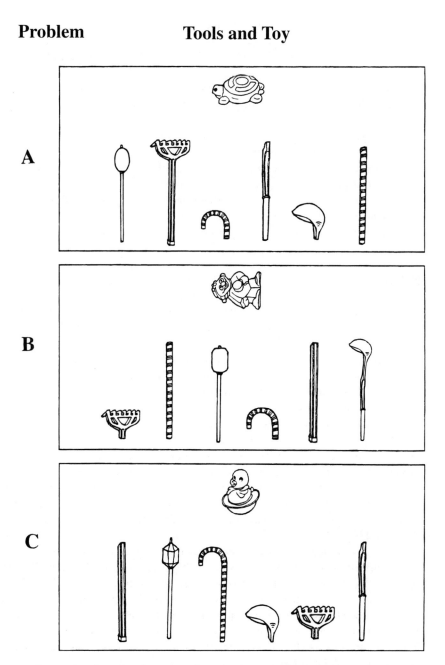

FIGURE 5.—Sets of tools presented on the three problems. Each set of tools and toy was presented equally often as the first problem (Problem A), the second problem (Problem B), and the third problem (Problem C).

Short tool 1: Shorter shaft, identical head, same color and pattern;

Short tool 2: Shorter shaft, identical head, different color and pattern.

These relations between the preceding target tool and the six new tools allowed us to examine the influence of both functional and perceptual characteristics on children's choices. If toddlers rely primarily on functional similarity between the target tool on the preceding problem and the potential tools on the new problem, they should choose the new target tool most often. If they are influenced by perceptual similarity, they should choose tools on the new problem with the same color and pattern as the previous target tool more often than the comparable alternatives that differ in color and pattern. If their choices are influenced by both functional and perceptual similarity, both of these patterns should be observed.

PROBLEMS

The toddlers were presented three parallel problems, which will be referred to as *Problem A*, *Problem B*, and *Problem C*, respectively. Each problem's label was determined by its order in the sequence of problems, rather than by the tools and toy that were available in it. Thus, whichever set of tools and toy a child encountered first was Problem A for that child. The particular set of tools that was present on a given problem was counterbalanced, so that on Problem A, the target tool for some children was the rake, for others the ladle, and for others the cane.

The tools and toys for the three problems sat atop three different tables in the room in which the experiment was conducted. Two of the tables were relatively tall; one was shorter. One of the tables had a gray top, one a white top, and one a woodgrain top. For the two problems on which the toy and tools were on a tall table, the child sat in the parent's lap; for the one problem with the short table, the child stood. The particular table that was used for each problem was counterbalanced, so that one third of children encountered each table on a given problem.

Children received five trials on Problem A, five on Problem B, and three on Problem C. Each trial represented a 1-min period during which the child had the opportunity to obtain the toy. In subsequent sections of this *Monograph*, we refer to each trial by a two-symbol label: the letter represents the problem and the number, the trial within the problem. Thus, Trial B3 was the third trial on Problem B, and Trial C2 was the second trial on Problem C.

To summarize, the three problems presented to each toddler varied in the toy that was being retrieved; the particular tools that were available for retrieving it; and contextual features, such as the height, shape, and color of the tables on which the toy and tools rested. The child, however, could use the same type of solution strategy on all of them.

EXPERIMENTAL CONDITIONS

The toddlers were randomly assigned to one of three experimental conditions. As shown in Table 1, these conditions varied only in what happened between the third and fourth trials of Problems A and B. In the modeling condition, after the third trial of Problems A and B, the experimenter told the child, "Let me show you how to get the toy." The experimenter then slowly demonstrated twice how to use the target tool to obtain the toy, waited a second or two, repeated the demonstrations, and then encouraged the child to "do what I did." If the child did not imitate the solution within 10 s, the experimenter repeated the sequence. Similarly, in the hint condition, after the third trial of Problems A and B, the experimenter pointed at the target tool and asked the child twice, "Can you use this to get Ernie?" If the child did not use any tool within 10 s, this hint was given twice more. The planned training was provided even if the child had already used a tool to solve the problem during the pretraining trials. Finally, in the control condition, children did not receive any training; they proceeded directly from the third to the fourth trial. Because children in the modeling and hint conditions received instruction between the third and fourth trials, we labeled the first three trials of each problem as *pretraining trials* and the fourth and fifth trials as *posttraining trials*. Thus, Trials A1–A3 were the three pretraining trials of Problem A, and Trials A4–A5 were the two posttraining trials of it.

PROCEDURE

When toddlers and parents arrived, they were greeted by a research assistant and escorted to a laboratory on the university campus. Approximately 10 min were allotted for the child and experimenter to interact until the child appeared comfortable in the new surroundings. At this point, testing began.

The child was directed to the first table, and, depending on which one it was, the child was asked either to stand in front of the table or to sit on the parent's lap, a few inches from it. For the two problems in which the child sat on the parent's lap, the parent was asked to prevent the child from climbing on the table. Before the first trial began, the parent was given sunglasses and asked to wear them to prevent any suggestive gaze. The parent also was asked not to gesture or say anything that might help the child solve the problem.

Until the beginning of each trial, a transparent box sat atop the toy and tools. Timing of the trial began when the experimenter lifted the box. Parents were asked to encourage their child to try hard on each trial, for example by saying, "Can you get that Ernie for Mommy?" or "You can do it." With one small class of exceptions, each trial ended when the child obtained the toy or when 1 min had elapsed, whichever came first. (The one class of exceptions came in the rare cases in which toddlers were in the middle of an attempt to get the toy when the allotted time expired. When this occurred, we allowed them to complete that attempt.) After each trial, the tools were rearranged on the table in a different left-to-right order, and the toy was returned to its original location. If a child failed to obtain the toy after Trial C3 (the last trial that was part of the experiment), the experimenter showed the child how to solve the problem by using the target tool and allowed the child to obtain it several times. The procedure lasted for 30–45 min, with a half minute interval between trials within a problem and a 2–3 min break between problems.

MEASURES

General strategy. Children's problem-solving activities were measured in several ways. One measure was the general strategy that children used on each trial. At this relatively general level, four strategies were distinguished. One was the tool strategy, defined as the child picking up any of the six tools and using it to reach for the toy. The second was the forward strategy. Here, children leaned forward, in an effort to reach the toy with their hands, or tried to climb on the table to get the toy but without a tool in their hand. The third general approach was the indirect strategy. This involved children asking their parent for help, looking toward the parent for help, or walking around the table to look at the toy from different angles. Finally, children fairly often looked at the toy but did not engage in any of these three types of activity; on these trials, they were classified as using no strategy. The indirect strategy was used on only around 10% of trials, but all three other strategies were used frequently.

In addition to these relatively common strategies, children occasionally used other approaches, such as attempting to combine two or more tools into one (à la Kohler's apes) or moving all tools out of the way to clear a path to the toy. These strategies, however, were used on fewer than 1% of trials and hence are not included in the analyses.

Specific tool-use strategies. Within the general strategy of using a tool, we differentiated among several specific tool strategies: using the target tool, using a tool that was too short, or using a tool with an ineffective head or no head. On some trials, children used more than one tool; when this occurred, they were credited with employing both specific tool strategies.

Success in obtaining toy. Use of a tool, even the target tool, did not guarantee success in obtaining the toy. Conversely, children sometimes obtained the toy when they used a tool other than the target. Therefore, we examined percentage of trials on which children obtained the toy. To provide a direct measure of strategy execution, we also analyzed percentage of successful use of the target tool (relative to percentage of trials on which the target tool was used successfully or unsuccessfully).

Solution time. Time to obtain the toy was also examined for those trials on which children obtained the toy. This provided another measure of the skill with which tools were used.

Our trial-by-trial assessment of children's general strategies, specific tool strategies, success in obtaining the toy, and solution time was based on performance on more than 1,000 trials. This extensive database allowed ample opportunity to examine the processes involved in toddlers' learning.

VI. OVERVIEW OF TODDLERS' PROBLEM SOLVING

EXAMPLES OF TODDLERS' PROBLEM SOLVING

To obtain a sense of what the toddlers' performance was like, consider the following two examples. (Recall that A1 refers to performance on the first trial of Problem A, A2 to performance on the second trial of Problem A, and so on.)

Example 1: A 31-month-old boy in the hint condition:

A1: No strategy.

A2: Indirect and forward strategies:
Child plays with tools but does not use them to reach for toy. After the experimenter again encourages him to get the toy, he asks his mom for help. Then he leans forward and stretches his arm toward the toy. When that does not work, he resumes playing with the tools without trying to obtain the toy.

A3: Forward, indirect, and tool strategies:
Child attempts to climb on table:
Mom: "Don't climb."
Child: "Mommy, you get it."
Mom: "You can get it. Can you show Mommy?"
Child tries to reach the toy;
Child: "I can't. My arm is too short."
Child looks at the tools, says "I can use this," picks up a tool with an ineffective head, but fails to retrieve the toy. Child continues to use the tool and finally retrieves the toy.

Instruction: The hint was given; then the child picked up the target tool and used it to obtain the toy.

A4 and A5: Tool strategy: Child uses the target tool and obtains the toy.

B1 to B5: Tool strategy: Child uses the target tool and obtains the toy.

C1: Tool strategy: Child uses the target tool and obtains the toy.

C2: Tool strategy: Child first picks up a tool without a head and fails to secure the toy. He then shifts to the target tool and pulls in the toy.

C3: Tool strategy: Child uses the target tool and obtains the toy.

Example 2: A 21-month-old girl in the modeling condition:

A1 and A2: Forward and indirect strategies: Child attempts to climb on the table to reach the toy and then turns to mom for help.

A3: No strategy.

Instruction: Child sees model and then uses the target tool to obtain the toy.

A4 and A5: Tool strategy: Child uses the target tool and obtains the toy.

B1: Tool strategy: Child picks up a tool without a head and fails to get the toy. Then child picks up the target tool but still fails to obtain the toy.

B2 and B3: Forward strategy.

Instruction: Child sees model and then uses the target tool to obtain the toy.

B4 and B5: Tool strategy: Child uses the target tool and obtains the toy.

C1: Tool strategy: Child chooses the target tool but fails to obtain the toy.

C2: Tool strategy: Child uses several ineffective tools and does not get the toy.

C3: Indirect strategy: Child asks her mother for help and does not obtain the toy.

These examples illustrate how children learned, or failed to learn, how to obtain the toy. In Example 1, when the boy first tried the tool strategy, he did not select the target tool. After receiving the hint, he used the target tool on Trials A4 and A5 and obtained the toy both times. When he encountered Problem B, he readily selected the target tool, even though it was perceptually different from the target tool on Problem A. He then transferred this effective approach to Problem C, though with one regression in which he chose an ineffective tool.

In Example 2, the girl reproduced the modeled strategy in the context of Problem A, the problem on which the modeling occurred. When she encountered the superficially different Problem B, however, she transferred the general strategy of using a tool but not the specific strategy of using the target tool. After seeing use of the target tool modeled on Problem B, she transferred both the general and the specific strategy (Trials C1 and C2), but she did not execute the tool strategy sufficiently well to obtain the toy. This child's performance highlights the fragility of newly acquired strategies. Even after beginning to use tools, she did not use the tool strategy consistently. Even when she used the target tool, she, like the boy in Example 1, did not use it very skillfully. Both inconsistent use of the newly acquired strategy and ineffective execution when it was used were characteristic of many toddlers' learning.

Having described qualitative aspects of toddlers' learning, we now turn to quantitative analyses. The results are reported in three sections. In the first section, we provide an overview of children's success in obtaining the toy, of the strategies that they used to do so, and of the amount of learning and transfer that occurred under different experimental conditions and at different ages. In the second section, we present a detailed analysis of the component processes that generated change over the three problems, over successive trials within a single problem, and within a given trial. In the third section, we examine individual differences in all of these aspects of strategic change.

LEARNING AND STRATEGY USE

The data in this section are organized to answer several relatively general questions. Are 1- and 2-year-olds capable of solving the toy-retrieval problem? Does seeing a model or receiving hints aid their learning? Can they transfer the learned strategy to novel problems? What strategies do they use, and how do these strategies change with experience? And how do older and younger toddlers differ along all of these dimensions?

Figure 6 illustrates the percentage of older and younger children in each condition who obtained the toy on each trial of each problem.

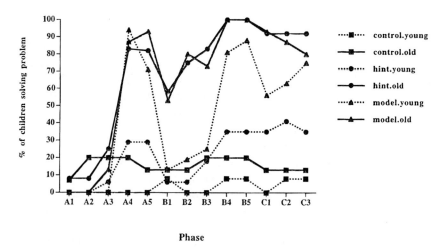

Phase

FIGURE 6.—Percentage of children in each age/condition group who obtained the toy on each of the 13 trials. The first three trials on each problem were pretraining trials; the last two trials on Problems A and B were posttraining trials.

Performance of children in all conditions on the pretraining trials of Problem A, and of children in the control condition throughout the experiment, makes a clear point: Without instruction, toddlers rarely were able to solve the toy-retrieval problem. Under such conditions, older toddlers obtained the toy on only about 15% of trials, and younger ones obtained it on about 5%.

Initial learning. To test whether modeling or the hint increased toddlers' success in obtaining the toy, we performed paired comparisons between their problem-solving performance before and after instruction on Problem A. Children who obtained the toy on at least one of the three pretraining trials of Problem A received a score of 1; others were scored 0. Similarly, children who obtained the toy on at least one of the two posttraining trials on Problem A received a score of 1; others received a score of 0. Despite this comparison being biased against showing learning (three pretraining trials, two posttraining trials), the analysis indicated that far more children solved Problem A after instruction than before. This was true in the modeling condition, $t(15) = 15.00$, $p < .0001$, and $t(14) = 7.48$, $p < .0001$, for younger and older children, respectively, and it was also true in the hint condition, $t(15) = 2.61$, $p < .05$, and $t(11) = 3.92$, $p < .005$, for younger and older children, respectively. In contrast, children in the control group did not differ on pretraining and posttraining trials of Problem A.

35

Transfer

Between-problem changes. A second general question concerned whether children were able to transfer what they learned on earlier problems to later ones. To examine this issue, we performed a 3 (problem: A, B, or C) × 3 (condition) × 2 (age) × 2 (sex) analysis of variance (ANOVA) on the number of times each child obtained the toy on the three pretraining trials of each problem. The key predictions regarding the pattern of transfer were that there should be a two-way interaction between problem and experimental condition and a three-way interaction among problem, condition, and age. On Problem A, children in all three conditions should be equally likely to solve pretraining trials, because they were treated identically up to that point. If children in the modeling and hint conditions transferred what they learned on Problem A to subsequent problems, however, they should be more likely than children in the control condition to obtain the toy on pretraining trials of Problems B and C. This would give rise to the interaction between condition and problem.

It also seemed likely that among children in the modeling and hint conditions, older toddlers would transfer what they had learned more completely and more quickly than younger toddlers. Thus, older children who received the modeling or hint should show especially enhanced performance on Problem B, relative to both older and younger children in the control condition and relative to younger children in the modeling and hint conditions. On the other hand, both older and younger children in the control condition were predicted to do equally poorly on all three problems. This would lead to the predicted three-way interaction among experimental condition, age, and problem.

Consistent with these predictions, there were significant interactions between condition and problem, $F(4, 148) = 14.96$, $p < .0001$, and among condition, problem, and age, $F(4, 148) = 2.49$, $p < .05$. Figure 6 makes clear the source of these interactions. First consider the performance of the older toddlers. Those in both the modeling and hint conditions transferred what they had learned from instruction on Problem A to the pretraining trials of Problem B (Trials B1, B2, and B3), thus leading to substantial improvements in pretraining performance from Problem A to Problem B (in the modeling condition, $t(14) = 6.44$, $p < .0001$; in the hint condition, $t(11) = 4.98$, $p < .001$). Older toddlers in both conditions obtained the toy even more often on the pretraining trials of Problem C than on those of Problem B (in the modeling condition, $t(14) = 2.47$, $p < .05$; in the hint condition, $t(11) = 3.22$, $p < .01$). In contrast, older toddlers in the control group showed no improvement over the three problems.

Younger toddlers in the modeling and hint conditions also transferred what they had learned, but they did so less quickly, and to a lesser extent, particularly in the hint condition. Those in the modeling condition tended to obtain the toy more often on the pretraining trials of Problem B than on the corresponding trials of Problem A, $t(15) = 2.06$, $p < .10$. They showed a large gain from the pretraining trials of Problem B to the corresponding trials of Problem C, $t(15) = 3.22$, $p < .01$. Younger toddlers in the hint condition did not show gains from Problem A to Problem B, but they did improve from the pretraining trials of Problem B to those of Problem C, $t(15) = 2.10$, $p < .05$. Thus, the three-way interaction reflected older toddlers in both the modeling and hint conditions showing considerable transfer on both Problems B and C; younger toddlers in the modeling condition showing some transfer on both Problems B and C; younger toddlers in the hint condition showing transfer only on Problem C; and both older and younger toddlers in the control condition showing no transfer.

The ANOVA also revealed a number of other main effects and interactions. Main effects were present for all four variables: Children in the modeling and hint conditions obtained the toy more often than those in the control condition, $F(2,74) = 24.82$, $p < .0001$; older children obtained the toy more often than younger children, $F(1,74) = 36.12$, $p < .0001$; boys obtained it more often than girls, $F(1,74) = 10.95$, $p < .001$; and children obtained it more often on Problems B and C than on Problem A, $F(2,148) = 65.62$, $p < .0001$. Among these findings, only the difference between boys and girls was unanticipated; boys obtained the toy on 32% of trials, whereas girls obtained it on 22%. The interaction between age and problem was also significant, $F(2,148) = 7.01$, $p < .005$. Except for the main effect for sex, all of these findings were best interpreted in the context of the condition by problem by age interaction described above.

Within-problem changes. In addition to the between-problem improvements in solutions following instruction, there also appeared to be improvements over the three pretraining trials within each problem. Such improvements were of interest because if they occurred, it would indicate that the learning of toddlers in the modeling and hint conditions was not entirely due to the instruction that they received after Trials A3 and B3. Rather, improvements over the pretraining trials of a given problem would indicate that the toddlers learned from their own problem-solving activities and their efforts to work out the lessons of the prior instruction.

An Age × Condition × Problem × Pretraining Trial (first, second, or third) ANOVA on number of children who solved the problem on each pretraining trial indicated a main effect for trial, $F(2,160) = 7.68$, $p < .001$, and a three-way interaction among age, problem, and trial, $F(4,160) = 3.01$, $p < .05$. Number of solutions generally increased from the first to the last pretraining trial, indicating that children were learning from their own problem-solving efforts. The interaction reflected the fact that this effect was limited to Problems B and C, and occurred earlier in the session for older toddlers than for younger ones. Older toddlers in the modeling and hint conditions increased their number of solutions between B1 and B3, matched-group $t(26) = 2.28$, $p < .05$. Among these children, 7 of 12 (58%) who did not obtain the toy on B1 did obtain it on B3. In contrast, far fewer older toddlers in the control group (1 of 13) showed such within-problem improvement from B1 to B3, $\chi^2(1) = 7.35$, $p < .01$. Younger toddlers in the modeling condition did not show much improvement on the pretraining trials of Problem B, but their success in obtaining the toy did tend to improve from the first to the last pretraining trial of Problem C, $t(15) = 1.86$, $p < .10$.

An interesting commonality was evident in the timing of the within-problem increase in solutions over the pretraining trials. These within-problem increases occurred at the same point in mastery for the three groups that showed the effect: older children in the modeling and hint conditions on Problem B and younger children in the modeling condition on Problem C. In all cases, in the group in which within-problem improvement occurred, performance was already at 50%–55% correct on the first pretraining trial of the new problem. In the groups that did not show such within-problem learning (older and younger children in the control group and younger children in the hint condition), pretraining performance never reached this high a level. The consistency suggests that instruction had to bring children to a moderate level of understanding before they could benefit from their own efforts to solve the problem.

Strategy use. One of the advantages of the tool-use task for studying strategy development was that it was easy to code the strategies. Two raters independently coded 104 trials (the performance of eight toddlers). Their ratings agreed on 100% of trials involving tool use, 97% of trials on which the forward strategy was used, and 95% of trials on which the indirect strategy was used. (In the few cases of disagreement, the classification was determined by discussion between the two raters.)

Changes in strategy use. Figure 7 shows the percentage of children who used each strategy on the three pretraining trials of each problem. Because children fairly often used both the tool strategy and the forward strategy on a single trial, the percentages in the three figures frequently sum to more than 100%.

The overlapping waves pattern that has been observed in studies of older children's cognitive development was clearly evident in the toddlers' pattern of strategic change. At first, most children used either no strategy or the forward strategy. Use of no strategy decreased considerably

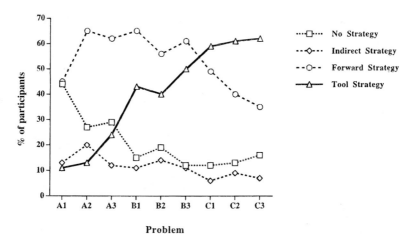

FIGURE 7.—Percentage of children who used each strategy on each pretraining trial.

after this. In contrast, use of the forward strategy increased; it was the most frequent strategy on the pretraining trials of Problems A and B. Its use gradually decreased, however, and the tool strategy supplanted it as the most common strategy by Problem C. The indirect strategy showed yet another pattern; toddlers used it occasionally throughout the experiment, but it never reached high levels of use.

Figure 8 breaks down strategy use by age and condition for the tool strategy (left panel), the forward strategy (middle panel) and no strategy (right panel) on the three pretraining trials of each problem. (The data for use of the indirect strategy are not shown, because this approach was used on only around 10% of trials.)

As shown in the left panel of Figure 8, use of tools to obtain the toys increased considerably over the three problems among both older and younger toddlers in the hint and modeling conditions. As shown in the middle panel, use of the forward strategy decreased considerably among older children in the hint and modeling conditions, but it remained high among younger ones in all conditions. As shown in the right panel, both older and younger toddlers in the hint and modeling conditions decreased the number of trials on which they used no strategy to obtain the toy. Finally, toddlers in the control condition did not change their use of any of these approaches very much over the three problems. As in the previous section on success in obtaining the toy, the changes in strategy use in the modeling and hint conditions were of very large magnitude, especially among the older toddlers. For example, older toddlers in the hint and modeling conditions used tools on only 20% of pretraining

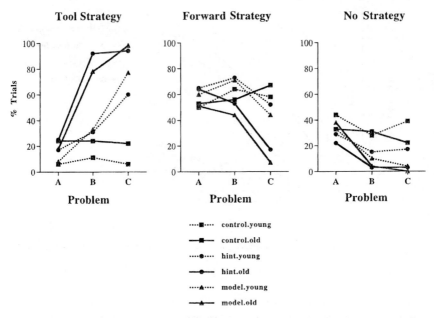

FIGURE 8.—Percentage of use of the three most common strategies on each problem by children in each age/condition group (pretraining trials).

trials on Problem A, but they used them on almost 100% of trials on Problem C.

We expected that changes in use of the tool strategy would parallel those involved in obtaining the toy. To test this hypothesis, we conducted a 3 (Condition) × 2 (Age) × 2 (Sex) × 3 (Problem) ANOVA, on percentage of use of the tool strategy on the pretraining trials of each problem. The analysis showed main effects for all four variables: condition, $F(2,74) = 26.51$, $p < .0001$; age, $F(1,74) = 19.48$, $p < .0001$; sex, $F(1,74) = 11.31$, $p < .005$; and problem, $F(2,148) = 76.00$, $p < .0001$. Children in the modeling and hint conditions used tools on more pretraining trials than did children in the control condition, older children used them more often than did younger ones, boys used them more frequently than did girls, and children in general used them more frequently on later than on earlier problems.

For the same reasons as in the analysis of frequency of obtaining the toy, the central predictions tested by this analysis of tool use on pretraining trials concerned the two-way interaction between problem and condition and the three-way interaction among problem, condition, and age. Both predicted interactions were present: the Condition × Problem interaction, $F(4,148) = 18.22$, $p < .0001$, and the Age × Condition × Problem interaction, $F(4,148) = 2.62$, $p < .05$. Furthermore, the interactions occurred for the predicted reasons. Both older and younger children in the modeling and hint conditions used tools increasingly often over problems, though the older children improved more quickly and to a somewhat greater extent. In contrast, neither older nor younger children in the control condition increased their use of tools over problems.

Post hoc analyses provided the following evidence for this interpretation. Both younger and older children in the modeling condition increased their use of the tool strategy from Problem A to Problem B, $t(15) = 2.67$, $p < .05$, for younger children, and $t(14) = 6.87$, $p < .0001$, for older children. They also increased their tool use from Problem B to Problem C, $t(15) = 3.52$, $p < .005$, for younger children, and $t(14) = 2.20$, $p < .05$, for older children. Older children in the hint condition increased their use of the tool strategy from Problem A to Problem B, $t(11) = 6.14$, $p < .0001$, but not from Problem B to Problem C. In contrast, younger children in the hint condition increased their use of tools later and to a lesser extent. As shown in the left panel of Figure 8, they increased their tool use a little from Problem A to Problem B, $t(15) = 1.82$, $p < .10$, but increased it considerably more from Problem B to Problem C, $t(15) = 3.22$, $p < .01$. Children at both age levels in the control condition failed to increase their use of the tool strategy over the three problems.

Thus, the reasons for the three-way interaction in the analysis of use of the tool strategy were the same as those underlying the three-way interaction in the analysis of success in obtaining the toy. Regardless of age or experimental condition, toddlers rarely used tools on the pretraining trials of Problem A. Both older and younger children in the control condition continued to rarely use tools on Problems B and C. Younger children in the modeling and hint conditions increased their use of tools on Problems B and C. Older children in the modeling and hint conditions increased their use of tools more quickly and to a greater extent than their younger peers.

Strategic variability. Along with this trend toward increasing use of the tool strategy was a great deal of strategic variability. This variability was evident in examination of individual toddlers' use of the four strategies (tool, forward, indirect, and no strategy). Among the 86 toddlers, 74% used either three or four strategies. Only three children, 3% of the sample, always used the same strategy. The mean number of strategies used by each child was 3.04. The forward strategy was used at least once by 98% of the children, the tool strategy by 76%, no strategy by 76%, and the indirect strategy by 53%. Thus, each of the four strategies was used by a majority of children at some time during the experiment.

41

Such a pattern might have been caused by the toddlers not discovering the one effective approach, the tool strategy, until they had tried the other three approaches, but then consistently using the tool strategy. This was not the case, however. Strategic variability continued after children began to use the tool strategy, though the degree of variability was greatly influenced by the instructional condition and the children's age. Among children in the control group, 11 of 12 who used the tool strategy also used other strategies on at least one trial after beginning to use the tool strategy. The younger toddlers in the control group used approaches other than the tool strategy on 84% of trials after the first time they used the tool strategy; the older toddlers in the control group did so on 48% of such trials. In contrast, children who received instruction in using the tool strategy subsequently used other approaches much less often. Younger toddlers in the modeling condition used approaches other than the tool strategy on 23% of trials after they started using the tool strategy; the corresponding percentage for younger toddlers in the hint condition was 20%. Even more extreme, after older toddlers in both the modeling and hint conditions started using the tool strategy, they used other approaches on only 4% of trials. Thus, instruction greatly reduced strategic variability, especially for the older toddlers, as well as promoting greater use of the tool strategy.

The increased use of the tool strategy greatly enhanced toddlers' ability to obtain the toy. There was considerably more to the story, however.

VII. COMPONENTS OF STRATEGIC CHANGE

Strategic change was hypothesized to include five components: initial acquisition, mapping, strengthening, refinement of choices, and increasingly skillful execution. Improvement in any of these five processes could increase overall speed and accuracy, even if no changes occurred in the other four. As it turned out, toddlers' learning involved improvements in all five components. Assessing these components separately allowed us to achieve a more precise conceptualization of the processes of learning and transfer on the toy retrieval task.[1]

ACQUISITION

A necessary first step in mastering the toy-retrieval task is to pick up a tool and attempt to get the toy with it. Whether a given child showed such acquisition was measured by whether the child used the tool strategy on at least 1 of the 13 trials. Success in obtaining the toy was not necessary, but the child needed at least to reach for the toy with the tool, rather than just waving it around.

Children in the three experimental conditions differed considerably in the likelihood of acquisition, $\chi^2(2) = 19.34$, $p < .0001$. Over the 13 trials, 100% of children in the modeling condition, 86% of children in the hint condition, and 56% of children in the control condition used the tool strategy at least once. The percentage of children who ever used

[1]Throughout this section, the total means on which the ANOVA are based, and which are used in the text, do not match the total means presented in the tables. For purposes of computing the ANOVAs, only those children who met the relevant criteria on all three problems were included; those means are given in the text. To communicate a sense of all children's performance, however, the total means in the tables were based on the performance of all children, even if they provided relevant data only on one or two problems. This also is the reason why the Ns for the ANOVAs are smaller than the total Ns in the tables.

the tool strategy was greater in the modeling condition than in the hint condition, $\chi^2(1) = 4.75$, $p < .05$, and it was greater in the hint condition than in the control condition, $\chi^2(1) = 6.06$, $p < .05$. On the other hand, there was no difference between the percentages of younger and older children who showed this initial acquisition (80% of younger children, 83% of older ones).

Considerably more boys than girls used the tool strategy at least once (91% of boys versus 72% of girls, $\chi^2(1) = 4.91$, $p < .05$). These sex differences were especially large in the control condition, in which children were encouraged to get the toy, and were told that they could use the tools to do so, but in which the experimenter did not direct them toward any particular strategy. In the control condition, 79% of boys but only 31% of girls used the tool strategy at least once, $\chi^2(1) = 6.24$, $p < .05$.

MAPPING

Mapping refers to the degree to which children who acquired the tool strategy on an earlier problem applied it to a subsequent problem without any training on that later problem. Recall that the three problems differed in the particular tools and toy that were presented, in the color and height of the table on which the tools and toy sat, and in the child's posture (sitting or standing) when trying to solve the problem.

To examine mapping, we first considered the conditional probability of children using the tool strategy on Trial B1, given that they earlier had used the tool strategy on Trial A4 or A5, and the conditional probability of their using the tool strategy on Trial C1, given that they had used it on Trial B4 or B5. The logic of using these conditional probabilities to assess mapping was that only children who acquired the tool strategy in the original situation could map what they had learned onto a novel context. The logic of only examining strategy use on the first trial of the new problem was that this allowed us to examine mapping of the tool strategy from the previous problem to the new problem, independent of learning over the three pretraining trials of the new problem. We limited the analysis to children in the two experimental groups, because few children in the control group used the tool strategy on Trial A4, A5, B4, or B5.

As shown in Table 2, of those toddlers who acquired the tool strategy on Problem A, about 60% mapped the strategy onto Problem B; of those who acquired it by Problem B, about 90% mapped it onto Problem C. The amount of mapping was quite similar for children in the modeling and hint conditions. This is a striking amount of transfer for toddlers, a population that until recently was viewed as being incapable of transfer (see Brown, 1990, for a discussion of past claims that toddlers were inca-

TABLE 2

Mapping of Tool Strategy Onto New Problems: P (Child used tool strategy on first pretraining trial of new problem | Child used tool strategy on one or both posttraining trials of previous problem)

Condition	Age (in months)	Conditional Probability of Mapping	
		A4 or A5 → B1[a]	B4 or B5 → C1
Modeling	18–26	.44	.80
	27–35	.71	1.00
Hint	18–26	.33	.78
	27–35	1.00	.92
Total[b]		.62 ($N = 47$)	.89 ($N = 51$)

[a]Numbers in the column A4 or A5 → B1 indicate the conditional probability that the child used the tool strategy on the first pretraining trial of Problem B, given that the child used the tool strategy on at least one of the two posttraining trials of Problem A. Thus, 44% of younger children in the modeling condition who used the tool strategy following training on Problem A transferred the strategy to the first pretraining trial of Problem B.

[b]Here and in subsequent tables, the numbers in the "Total" row do not equal the mean of the numbers above them in the column, because the numbers higher in the column are based on different numbers of observations for older and younger children in each condition. Instead, the numbers in the Total row are based on observations of all children who used the tool strategy on the previous posttraining problem.

pable of transfer and for additional evidence that they can transfer what they have learned to new problems and situations).

To better understand factors that influenced mapping of the tool strategy onto new problems and contexts, we conducted a 2 (condition: modeling or hint) × 2 (age) × 2 (sex) × 2 (problem: B or C) ANOVA. Only those children in the experimental conditions who used the tool strategy on posttraining trials of both Problems A and B were included in this analysis ($N = 47$). Children who used the tool strategy on the first trial of the new problem received a score of 1 for that problem; children who did not use it on the first trial of the new problem received a score of 0 for that problem. The ANOVA showed main effects for age, $F(1,39) = 14.26$, $p < .001$, and problem, $F(1,39) = 14.73$, $p < .001$, and an interaction between age and problem, $F(1,39) = 4.34$, $p < .05$. The three-way interaction among age, condition, and problem was also marginally significant, $F(1,39) = 2.88$, $p < .10$.

Paired comparisons revealed that in the modeling condition, the amount of mapping of the tool strategy to a novel problem increased from Problem B to Problem C. This was true for both younger children, $t(14) = 2.09$, $p = .05$, and older ones, $t(13) = 2.28$, $p < .05$. Among the younger children in the hint condition, amount of mapping of the tool strategy to Problem C was also greater than to Problem B, $t(6) = 2.83$, $p < .05$. Older children in the hint condition were already at 100% mapping on Problem B, and thus could not show any increase over problems. In

45

general, however, the 1- and 2-year-olds exhibited even more mapping of the tool strategy onto Problem C than onto Problem B.

STRENGTHENING

Generating a novel strategy is the beginning of the strategy development process, but it is not the end. Even the most advantageous new strategies need to be strengthened, so that they are used consistently when they are applicable. Such consistency needs to be gained both in the context of initial acquisition and in new contexts to which the strategy is mapped.

One measure of the degree of strengthening of the tool strategy was how consistently it was used on a given problem once it had been used for the first time on that problem. As in the analyses of initial acquisition and mapping, this analysis was performed on the pretraining trials of each problem. Table 3 shows the conditional probability of using the tool strategy on a later pretraining trial, given that it had been used on an earlier pretraining trial on the same problem. Note that only children who started using the tool strategy on the first or second trial of each problem could be included in this analysis, because there were no pretraining trials following the third trial on each problem.

To test whether consistency of use of the tool strategy increased over the three problems, a one-way ANOVA was performed on the data of toddlers who used the tool strategy on the first or second trial on all three problems ($N = 10$). The ANOVA revealed a main effect for problem, $F(2,18) = 3.97$, $p < .05$. This effect was due to consistency of use of

TABLE 3

Consistency of Use of Tool Strategy: P (Tool strategy used on a
pretraining trial of a problem | Tool strategy used on the immediately
previous pretraining trial of that problem)

Condition	Age (mo.)	Problem A	Problem B	Problem C
Hint	18–26	.67	.91	.86
	27–35	.50	1.00	.96
Modeling	18–26	.00	.50	.86
	27–35	1.00	.92	.97
Total		.63 ($N = 15$)	.82 ($N = 43$)	.90 ($N = 57$)

Note.—Control group was not included because the number of children using the tool strategy was too low. The means reflect consistency of use of all children in these groups, not only of those who used the tool strategy on one of the first two trials of all three problems.

46

the tool strategy increasing over the three problems (55%, 85%, and 95%, on Problems A, B, and C, respectively).

Another reflection of the strength of a strategy is its accessibility. In the present context, the accessibility of the tool strategy was measured by the percentage of pretraining trials on which it was the first approach attempted, relative to the total number of trials on which it was used anytime during the trial (Table 4). Thus, an increase in accessibility meant that children more often were using the tool strategy as their first strategy on a trial, rather than as a later strategy.

To test whether the accessibility of the tool strategy increased over problems, a one-way ANOVA was conducted on the performance of those children who used the strategy at least once on all three problems ($N = 23$). The ANOVA revealed a main effect for problem, $F(2,44) = 6.25$, $p < .005$. The percentage of tool-use trials that children began by using the tool strategy increased from 43% on Problem A to 62% on Problem B to 83% on Problem C. Paired t tests indicated increases from Problem A to Problem C, $t(22) = 3.18$, $p < .005$, and from Problem B to Problem C, $t(22) = 2.28$, $p < .05$. Thus, not only were there substantial increases in the likelihood of using a tool at all; the likelihood of using a tool first, rather than later, also increased considerably.

It also was possible that the accessibility of the tool strategy would increase over trials within a given problem, as well as between problems. This would occur if the children's own efforts to solve a given problem led to their learning that using tools was a good idea on that problem. To test this possibility, we performed separate one-way ANOVAs on accessibility of the tool strategy among children who used the tool strategy on all three pretraining trials of Problem B ($N = 28$) and those who used it on all three pretraining trials of Problem C ($N = 44$). The ANOVA on within-problem changes in accessibility of the tool strategy on Problem B

TABLE 4

ACCESSIBILITY OF TOOL STRATEGY: P (TOOL STRATEGY WAS FIRST STRATEGY USED ON A GIVEN PRETRAINING TRIAL | TOOL STRATEGY USED AT SOME POINT ON THAT TRIAL)

Condition	Age (mo.)	Problem A	Problem B	Problem C
Hint	18–26	.28	.50	.61
	27–35	.50	.58	.92
Modeling	18–26	.25	.79	.81
	27–35	.40	.77	.98
Total		.48 ($N = 27$)	.68 ($N = 49$)	.85 ($N = 59$)

NOTE.—This table includes data for all children, even if the child did not use the tool strategy on pretraining trials on all three problems.

showed a main effect for trial order, $F(2,54) = 4.59$, $p < .05$. Among children who used the tool strategy on all three pretraining trials of Problem B, the tool strategy was the first one used by 57% of children on Trial B1, 75% on B2, and 89% on B3. Paired comparisons indicated that strategy accessibility on B3 was higher than on B1, $t(27) = 3.10$, $p < .005$. The corresponding ANOVA for Problem C revealed no differences in accessibility across the three pretraining trials. This appeared to be due to ceiling effects. Among toddlers who used the tool strategy on all three trials, the tool strategy was the first one used by 82% of children on C1, 93% on C2, and 87% on C3. Thus, the tool strategy was sufficiently strong by Problem C that it was used first by the large majority of toddlers from the initial presentation of the new problem. More generally, these findings meant that the instructional procedures (the hint and modeling) were not the only factors responsible for the increasing strength of the tool strategy; the toddlers' own problem-solving efforts also contributed.

Using a tool is different than choosing the right tool, however. Therefore, we next examined children's choices among the six tools that they encountered on each problem.

REFINEMENT OF STRATEGY CHOICES

As often occurs, strategy choice on the toy-retrieval task was a hierarchical process. To have a good chance of succeeding, the toddlers needed not only to choose the tool strategy; within the set of tools, they needed to choose the target tool, the one tool among the six that was long enough to reach the toy and that had a head at a right angle to the shaft. Analyses of refinement of choices among the tools showed that it was a surprisingly complex process.

A graphical presentation of the results helps to convey the multifaceted changes that occurred during the course of the experiment. The six graphs in Figure 9 illustrate for each age-condition group both the overall changes in frequency of tool use and the refinements in the type of tool that was chosen on the pretraining trials of each problem. On Problem A, before children in any condition received training, they rarely used any tool. This continued to be the case for children in the control condition on Problems B and C. On those later problems, however, children in the hint and modeling conditions considerably increased their use of tools in general and increasingly often chose the target tool on those trials on which they used a tool.

An Age × Problem × Condition × Sex ANOVA on frequency of use of the target tool on the three pretraining trials of each problem provided statistical evidence for these statements and revealed some additional effects as well. The analysis showed main effects for all four variables: condition, $F(2,74) = 31.55$, $p < .0001$; age, $F(1,74) = 20.47$, $p < .0001$; sex, $F(1,74) = 10.14$, $p < .005$; and problem, $F(2,148) = 54.31$, $p < .0001$. Children in the modeling and hint conditions used the target tool more frequently than children in the control condition, older children used it more frequently than younger ones, boys used it more frequently than girls, and children used it more frequently on later than on earlier problems.

The ANOVA also yielded interactions that paralleled those in the analyses of frequency of obtaining the toy and frequency of using a tool. There was a condition by problem interaction, $F(4,148) = 14.35$, $p < .0001$, and a tendency toward an age by condition by problem interaction, $F(4,148) = 2.12$, $p < .10$. Again, the interactions occurred for the predicted reasons. Both older and younger toddlers increased their use of the target tool greatly in the modeling and hint conditions, older toddlers in those conditions improved more quickly and to a somewhat greater extent than younger ones, and neither older nor younger toddlers in the control condition improved over problems.

This overview of changes in use of the target tool sets the stage for a series of analyses that addressed four specific issues about the choice refinement process: (a) Did the toddlers bring to the experiment knowledge of tools that constrained and guided their subsequent choices? (b) What changes beyond that initial knowledge occurred over the three problems? (c) What types of refinements in strategy choices occurred over the three pretraining trials within a given problem? and (d) What types of refinements in strategy choices did toddlers make within a given trial?

Knowledge about tools prior to instruction. Analysis of choices of tools on the pretraining trials of Problem A allowed us to examine what toddlers knew about the properties of effective tools before they received any instruction. This knowledge seemed important, because if the toddlers entered the experiment already having a sense of the properties of effective tools, this knowledge may have helped them draw the intended lesson from the instruction that they subsequently received.

The toddlers' choices among the six tools on the pretraining trials of Problem A indicated that they indeed did enter the experiment with some understanding of the requisites of effective tools. Because toddlers used tools on only about 20% of these trials, and because all children were presented identical experience up to this point in the experiment, we combined the data across conditions and ages. First we examined percentage of choice of tools with shafts long enough to reach the toy. Of the six tools, four (67%) met this criterion. Children chose these long tools, however, on 93% of trials on which they chose any tool, more than if they

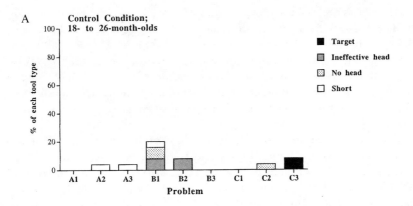

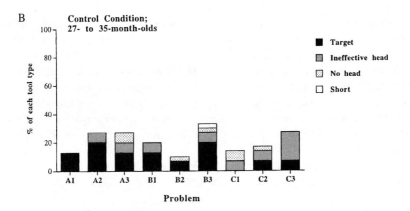

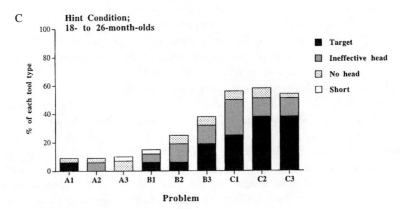

FIGURE 9.—*Figure continues on facing page.*

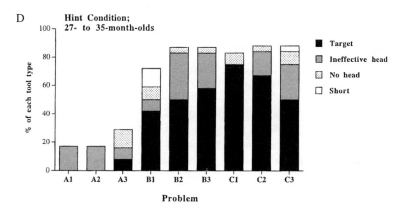

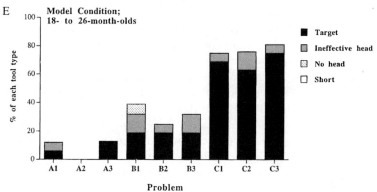

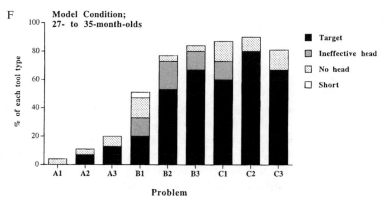

FIGURE 9.—Percentage of pretraining trials in each age/condition group in which each type of tool was chosen first. The distance between the height of each bar and 100% indicates the percentage of trials on which an approach other than the tool strategy was used first. (A) 18- to 26-month-olds in the control condition; (B) 27- to 35-month-olds in the control condition; (C) 18- to 26-month-olds in the hint condition; (D) 27- to 35-month-olds in the hint condition; (E) 18- to 26-month-olds in the modeling condition; (F) 27- to 35-month-olds in the modeling condition.

had chosen randomly, $t(40) = 6.24$, $p < .0001$. Within the group of long tools, two had heads and two did not; children more often chose tools with heads (66% of choices) than the 50% chance probability, $t(37) = 2.02$, $p < .05$. Then we examined whether on those trials on which children chose a tool with a head, they were more likely than chance to choose the tool with the most effective head, the target tool. They were not; their choices here did not differ from chance. Thus, before instruction, toddlers already tended to choose tools that were long enough to reach the toy and that had heads that might be useful for pulling the toy to them, but they did not seem to differentiate between tools with more and less useful heads.

Refinement of choices over problems. The second set of issues regarding the toddlers' choices among the six tools involved changes that occurred from Problem A to Problem B to Problem C. We first examined whether the increased use of the target tool over problems was entirely attributable to increased use of tools in general, or whether children's choices among the six tools also became more refined. To examine this issue, we computed each child's conditional probability of using the target tool first on the pretraining trials, given that the child used some tool on the trial. If children's choices among the tools became more refined with age and with experience on the task, we would expect that even when we limited the analysis to trials on which children used some tool, the percentage of trials on which the target tool was chosen first would increase. Because tool use was relatively rare on Problem A in all three conditions, and because it continued to be relatively rare in the control condition on Problems B and C, we limited this analysis to performance on Problems B and C of children in the modeling and hint conditions who used a tool on at least one pretraining trial of both problems.

A 2 (condition: modeling or hint) × 2 (problem: B or C) × 2 (age) × 2 (sex) ANOVA ($N = 39$) yielded main effects for problem, $F(1,31) = 4.87$, $p < .05$, and condition, $F(1,31) = 4.56$, $p < .05$. The percentage of tool use trials on which the target tool was the first tool chosen increased from 52% on Problem B to 71% on Problem C. Because there were six tools, only one of which was the target, this meant that children's choices among the tools were already much better than chance on Problem B, and that the choices became yet more refined on Problem C. Children in the modeling condition chose the target tool first on 69% of tool-use trials, whereas children in the hint condition chose the target tool first on 53% of such trials. Unlike the case with overall frequency of use of the target tool, older children did not choose the target tool on a higher percentage of tool-use trials than younger children, nor did boys choose it on a higher percentage of such trials than girls.

These results raised the converse issue to the one that motivated the just-described analysis: Were changes in overall tool use totally due to changes in use of the target tool? To find out, we analyzed the number of trials on which children used a tool other than the target tool. The Age × Sex × Condition × Problem ANOVA showed that all four variables influenced frequency of using tools other than the target tool. Main effects were present for age, $F(1,74) = 5.04$, $p < .05$, sex, $F(1,74) = 4.77$, $p < .05$, condition, $F(2,74) = 6.92$, $p < .01$, and problem, $F(2,148) = 5.10$, $p < .01$. Older children used tools other than the target tool on 22% of trials, younger children on 12%. Boys used them on 21% of trials, versus 13% for girls. Frequency of use of tools other than the target increased from 10% to 21% to 22% from Problem A to B to C. Toddlers in the hint condition used tools other than the target more often than toddlers in either the modeling or control conditions (28% versus 16% and 9%, respectively). Thus, although children in both the modeling and hint conditions increased their use of tools to a similar extent, frequency of use of the target tool increased more in the modeling condition, whereas frequency of use of nontarget tools increased more in the hint condition. This made sense, because toddlers in the modeling condition saw the target tool being used to pull in the toy, whereas those in the hint condition saw the experimenter point to the target tool but did not see it used. Thus, in the hint condition, it may have been more difficult to remember which tool was the target.

The fact that, over problems, choices of tools were increasingly influenced by functional aspects of the tools does not imply that superficial similarity to previous target tools played no role in subsequent choices. Recall that the six potential tools on each problem included two short tools and two long tools without heads. Within each pair, the only difference between the two tools was that one had the same pattern and color as the target tool on the previous problem (Figure 5). To determine whether children's choices among tools were affected by these superficial similarities, we examined whether children were more likely to use the two nonoptimal tools with superficial features identical to those of the previous target tool than the two nonoptimal tools with different superficial features.

Because children did not choose any of these nonoptimal tools very often, we combined the data over age groups and over the modeling and hint conditions (children in the control condition were not included because they rarely learned which object was the target tool and therefore could not learn its superficial features). Also, because memory for the superficial aspects of the target tool from the previous problem was likely to fade, we limited this analysis to the first choice of tool on Trial B1 and Trial C1. On Trial B1, 15% of children who used the tool strategy used

53

one of the two nonoptimal tools that were superficially similar to the target tool on Problem A. In comparison, only 3% of children chose one of the two matched comparison tools that were not superficially identical to the previous target tool, $t(71) = 2.59$, $p < .05$. On Problem C1, the comparable percentages were 5% and 3% (ns). Thus, superficial similarity did influence initial choices of tools on Problem B, but by Problem C, the toddlers' choices among tools were influenced only by functional similarity.

Refinement of choices within problems. The third issue regarding refinement of strategy choices concerned whether there were refinements over the three pretraining trials within a given problem. To examine whether the toddlers showed such within-problem learning, separate one-way ANOVAs were conducted on percentage of use of the target tool among children who used the tool strategy on all three pretraining trials of Problem B ($N = 28$) and those who used the tool strategy on all three trials of Problem C ($N = 44$). The first ANOVA showed a main effect for trial order within Problem B, 39% use of the target tool on tool use trials on B1, 57% on B2, and 68% on B3, $F(2,54) = 3.57$, $p < .05$. Paired comparisons indicated that percentage of use of the target tool on the third trial was higher than on the first trial, $t(27) = 2.52$, $p < .05$. The parallel ANOVA on Problem C did not reveal differences in likelihood of choosing the target tool, rather than just some tool, across the three pretraining trials (64%, 73%, and 68% choices of the target tool on tool-use trials on C1, C2, and C3, respectively). These results indicate that children did indeed learn through their problem-solving experience to choose the target tool increasingly often over the pretraining trials of Problem B. They then maintained the same high frequency of choices of the target tool as they had reached by Trial B3 (around 70%) on all trials of Problem C.

Refinement of choices within individual trials. The fourth issue was whether children shifted their choices of tools in adaptive directions within individual trials. That is, on trials on which children started a trial by using an ineffective tool, did they disproportionately switch to the target tool? Such adaptive changes within trials would again attest to children learning from their own problem-solving efforts, as there was no instruction within any trial. The data were combined over ages and conditions because the number of within-trial shifts from one tool to another was relatively small.

The chance likelihood that a child who shifted away from an ineffective tool would choose the target tool was 20% (one of the five remaining tools was the target). On Problem B, 42% of within-trial shifts away from ineffective tools were to the target tool, more than the 20% that would have been expected by chance, $t(35) = 2.60$, $p < .01$. On Problem C, an even higher percentage of shifts, 63%, were from ineffective tools to the target. This again was more than would have been expected by chance, $t(29) = 4.84$, $p < .001$. Thus, the toddlers' strategy choices became more refined within individual trials, as they did over the three problems and over the pretraining trials within each problem.

EFFECTIVENESS OF EXECUTION

In addition to acquiring and strengthening new strategies, mapping them onto novel problems, and refining choices among alternative approaches, children also often need to improve their execution of new strategies. In the present context, improvements in both accuracy and speed were necessary before toddlers could consistently obtain the toy.

Success in obtaining the toy. To determine whether execution of the tool strategy became more effective with experience, we examined changes over the three problems in children's conditional probability of obtaining the toy, given that they used a tool on the trial. The analysis included only those children who used the tool strategy at least once on each of the three problems, and included only pretraining trials of each problem. As shown in Table 5, the percentage of tool-use trials on which children obtained the toy increased substantially over the three problems, $F(2,44) = 14.60$, $p < .0001$. Paired t tests indicated that success in obtaining the toy on trials on which a tool was used increased from Problem A to B, $t(22) = 3.16$, $p < .005$, and from Problem B to C, $t(22) = 2.37$, $p < .05$.

We also examined whether execution of the tool strategy improved within problems. The issue was the same as in the previously described

TABLE 5

EFFECTIVENESS OF EXECUTION OF TOOL STRATEGY:
P(TOY OBTAINED | CHILD USED A TOOL)

Condition	Age (mo.)	Problem A	Problem B	Problem C
Control	18–26	0	.25	1.00
	27–35	.53	.50	.40
Hint	18–26	.08	.36	.61
	27–35	.50	.79	.94
Modeling	18–26	0	.45	.76
	27–35	.27	.81	.93
Total		.26 ($N = 27$)	.61 ($N = 49$)	.79 ($N = 59$)

analysis of within-problem refinements in choices among the tools: Did children learn from their own problem-solving efforts, as well as from the instruction that the experimenter provided? One-way ANOVAs were conducted on the performance of children who used the tool strategy on all three pretraining trials of Problem B ($N = 28$) and Problem C ($N = 44$). (There were too few tool-use trials on Problem A for the analysis to be meaningful there.) The ANOVA for Problem B showed a tendency for increased success over trials in obtaining the toy: 71% successful execution of the tool strategy on B1 and 86% on B2 and B3, $F(2,54) = 2.40$, $p < .10$. The ANOVA for Problem C revealed no differences in percentage of successful execution across the three pretraining trials (86%, 87%, and 93%, respectively). As in the within-problem improvements in choices among tools, toddlers' execution of the tool strategy tended to improve over the pretraining trials of Problem B, and it stayed at that high level throughout Problem C.

Part of the improvement in execution of the tool strategy was attributable to the increasingly refined strategy choices that were described in the previous section. When children used the target tool, they were far more likely to obtain the toy than when they used other tools (although they sometimes were successful in obtaining the toy with other long tools). We wanted to know whether children also improved the skill with which they wielded the optimal tool. To find out, we examined children's success in obtaining the toy on those trials on which they chose the target tool. Given that few children in any condition used the target tool on the pretraining trials of Problem A, and few children in the control condition ever used it, we compared percentage of successful use of the target tool on Problems B and C of children in the modeling and hint conditions. Only the 27 children who used the target tool on pretraining trials of both Problem B and Problem C were included in the analysis.

The Age × Condition × Sex × Problem ANOVA yielded main effects for problem, $F(1,19) = 8.04$, $p < .01$, and age, $F(1,19) = 17.44$, $p < .0001$, and an interaction between age and problem, $F(1,19) = 6.75$, $p < .05$. As shown in Table 6, older toddlers almost always obtained the toy when they used the target tool on either problem, but younger ones improved from Problem B to Problem C in their effectiveness in obtaining the toy when they used the target tool. Thus, the toddlers' greater success in obtaining the toy on Problem C than on Problem B was due not only to their choosing the target tool more often but also to the younger toddlers becoming more skillful in using it.

Speed of obtaining the toy. Effectiveness of execution of the tool strategy also improved with problem-solving experience in a second sense: the speed with which children obtained the toy. Mean solution time for chil-

TABLE 6

Effectiveness of Execution When Target Tool Was Used:
P(Toy obtained | Child used target tool)

Condition	Age (mo.)	Problem B	Problem C
Hint	18–26	.57	.76
	27–35	.90	.96
Modeling	18–26	.75	.91
	27–35	1.00	1.00
Total		.76 ($N = 30$)	.87 ($N = 49$)

dren in the modeling and hint conditions on trials on which the toy was obtained is presented in Figure 10. To provide statistical evidence for the improvement in problem-solving speed with experience, we conducted a one-way ANOVA on mean solution time for each problem. Only children who obtained the toy on at least one pretraining trial on all three problems were included in the analysis ($N = 7$). The ANOVA revealed a main effect for problem, $F(2,12) = 7.33$, $p < .01$. The toddlers' mean solution times was 33 s on Problem A, 15 s on Problem B, and 12 s on Problem C. Paired t tests indicated that solution time decreased from Problem A to B, $t(6) = 2.89$, $p < .05$, and from Problem A to C, $t(6) = 2.75$, $p < .05$.

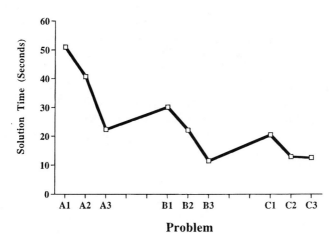

Figure 10.—Mean solution time (s) of children in the modeling and hint conditions on trials on which the toy was obtained.

We also wanted to determine whether speed of obtaining the toy improved over the pretraining trials within a given problem. As in the previous analysis of within-problem performance, the purpose was to see if children learned from their own problem-solving efforts. To find out, we performed one-way ANOVAs comparing solution times on the three trials of children who obtained the toy on all three pretraining trials on Problem B ($N = 18$) and Problem C ($N = 36$). The ANOVA on Problem B showed that times decreased over the three trials, means of 15 s, 10 s, and 10 s on B1, B2, and B3, respectively, $F(2,34) = 11.62$, $p < .0001$. Paired comparisons indicated that solution time decreased from the first trial to the second, $t(17) = 3.04$, $p < .005$, and from the first trial to the third, $t(17) = 4.48$, $p < .001$. The ANOVA on Problem C also indicated that solution times decreased over the three trials, 21 s, 11 s, and 11 s, respectively, $F(2,70) = 9.09$, $p < .001$. Paired comparisons indicated that solution time decreased from C1 to C2 and from C1 to C3, $t(35) = 3.36$, $p < .005$, and $t(35) = 3.10$, $p < .005$, respectively.

These improvements in solution time were not attributable to increased use of the target tool on later problems and on later trials. When only the solution time associated with the target tool was examined, a similar pattern was obtained: Mean solution time decreased from 32 s for Problem A to 18 s for Problem B to 14 s for Problem C (means based on all uses of target tool). A paired t test was performed on the 22 children who obtained the toy with the target tool on at least one pretraining trial on both Problems B and C. The mean solution time decreased from 19 s to 12 s from Problem B to C, $t(21) = 2.73$, $p < .05$.

To summarize, improvements in toddlers' performance on the toy-retrieval task reflected all five of the hypothesized components of strategic change: (a) acquiring the strategy of using a tool to obtain the toy; (b) mapping the strategy onto novel problems; (c) strengthening the tool strategy, so that it was used consistently; (d) more refined choices among the tools (greater use of the target tool); and (e) executing the tool strategy increasingly skillfully. The degree to which each of these components was mastered varied with children's age and with the type of instruction they were given. There also were substantial individual differences in children's learning, even among those in the same experimental condition. We now turn to them.

VIII. INDIVIDUAL DIFFERENCES IN LEARNING

The microgenetic design used in this study allowed detailed analysis of changes in individual children's performance. Given that cognitive change was largely limited to the modeling and hint conditions, the analyses of individual patterns of change focused on children in those two conditions.

CHANGES IN STRATEGY USE

Table 7 illustrates the percentage of older and younger children in the modeling and hint conditions who showed three common patterns of strategic change. The small figures at the top of the table indicate that one common pattern was increasing use of tools and decreasing use of the forward strategy, that a second common pattern was increasing use of tools and simultaneous frequent use of the forward strategy, and that a third common pattern was little use of tools throughout the experiment.

As shown in the leftmost column of numbers in Table 7, absolute majorities of older toddlers in the hint condition and both older and younger toddlers in the modeling condition showed the first pattern. These were children who progressed from little tool use on Problem A to consistent tool use by Problem C. Although this pattern was common among older children in the modeling and hint conditions and among younger children in the modeling condition, it was quite uncommon among younger children in the hint condition; only 25% of them showed it.

Instead, most younger children in the hint condition showed one of two other patterns. As shown in the rightmost column of Table 7, almost 40% of them did not learn the tool strategy; they did not use a tool on more than one pretraining trial on any of the three problems. The third pattern, shown by quite a few of the younger children in the hint condition as well as by some others, was for the forward strategy to be common throughout the experiment and for the tool strategy also to become

TABLE 7

PERCENTAGE OF TODDLERS SHOWING EACH PATTERN OF CHANGE IN USE
OF TOOL AND FORWARD STRATEGIES ON PRETRAINING TRIALS

		Tool strategy up Forward strategy down[a]	Tool strategy up Forward strategy high	Tool strategy low throughout
Condition	Age (mo.)	Percentage of Children Showing Pattern		
Hint	18–26	25	25	38
	27–35	67	17	0
Modeling	18–26	69	6	0
	27–35	87	0	0

[a]Use of tool strategy represented in schematic diagrams by squares; use of forward strategy represented by diamonds. Criteria for inclusion in tools-strategy-up/forward-strategy-down group were at least two more uses of tool strategy on pretraining trials of Problem C than Problem A, and no more than one use of forward strategy on Problem C. Criteria for inclusion in tools-strategy-up/forward-strategy-high group were at least two more uses of tool strategy on pretraining trials of Problem C than on Problem A, but also at least two uses of forward strategy on the three pretraining trials of Problem C. Criteria for inclusion in tools-strategy-low group were no more than one use of tool strategy on the pretraining trials of any problem. The percentages in each age/condition group do not add up to 100% because not all children fit any of the three patterns.

common by Problem C. Thus, these children used both the forward strategy and the tool strategy on most trials of Problem C.

CHANGES IN USE OF TARGET TOOL

The optimal strategy in this experiment was for children consistently to choose the target tool first. Pronounced individual differences were again evident in whether this goal was attained and in the path that led to it when it was attained. The columns in Table 8 are ordered from the slowest and least complete learning in the leftmost column to the fastest and most complete learning in the rightmost column. As shown in the leftmost column, a substantial majority of younger toddlers in the hint condition rarely if ever chose the target tool first on any pretraining problem. As shown in the next column, quite a few of the toddlers in all four age/condition groups, especially younger toddlers in the modeling condition, showed late learning. They rarely used the target tool first on the

TABLE 8

PERCENTAGE OF TODDLERS SHOWING EACH PATTERN OF CHANGE IN USE
OF TARGET TOOL AS FIRST TOOL ON PRETRAINING TRIALS

		No learning	Late learning	Continuous learning	Quick learning

Condition	Age (mo.)	Percentage of Children Showing Pattern			
		No learning	Late learning	Continuous learning	Quick learning
Hint	18–26	69	25	6	0
	27–35	25	25	25	25
Modeling	18–26	31	38	6	0
	27–35	20	20	33	13

NOTE.—The criterion for inclusion in the No Learning group was that the child not use the target tool more than once on the pretraining trials of any problem. Criteria for inclusion in the Late Learning group were that the child not use the target tool on more than one pretraining trial on either Problem A or B, but that the child use it on at least two trials of Problem C. The criteria for inclusion in the Continuous Learning group were that the child use the target tool on more trials on Problem B than on Problem A and on more trials still on Problem C. Finally, the criteria for inclusion in the Quick Learning group were that the child use the target tool on at least two more pretraining trials on Problem B than Problem A, and that the child use the target tool on at least as many pretraining trials on Problem C as on Problem B. As in Table 7, the percentages do not always add to 100%, because some children showed patterns that did not meet any of these criteria.

pretraining trials of Problems A and B, but they did so often on Problem C. A number of toddlers, primarily older ones, showed continuous learning. They increased their use of the target tool somewhat from Problem A to Problem B and further on Problem C. Finally, a few of the toddlers, again primarily older ones, showed quick learning; they consistently chose the target tool as their first approach on both Problem B and Problem C. Table 8 as a whole reveals quite striking differences between the rapidity with which older and younger toddlers learned: 48% of older toddlers, but only 3% of younger ones, increased their choice of the target tool as the initial approach from Problem A to Problem B.

DISTAL AND PROXIMAL INFLUENCES ON LEARNING

Most analyses of individual differences in problem solving examine how well distal variables such as age, sex, prior knowledge, and training condition predict which children will succeed in solving the problem (e.g., Johnson & Mervis, 1994; Schneider, Korkel, & Weinert, 1989). The present study supplemented analyses of the roles of these distal variables with measures of proximal processes (the five components described above). Measuring both distal and proximal influences allowed us to test the degree to which the distal characteristics exerted their contribution through influencing execution of proximal processes early in the learning sequence, which in turn influenced proximal processes later in the sequence. Possessing both types of information also allowed us to determine the degree to which the distal processes exerted direct influences on the later proximal processes, above and beyond those they exerted on the earlier proximal processes.

In some cases, the measures of proximal processes are not identical to those previously utilized to assess the components. This reflected the need in the present analysis to assess each component in a single measure that clearly separated the components. Given that only some of the relations between the distal and proximal influences on learning were theoretically specified, we performed stepwise regression analyses. All results are reported with adjusted R squares. In addition, a correlation matrix including all the distal and proximal variables involved in the componential analyses is provided in Table 9.

We first examined distal predictors of success in obtaining the toy among the 59 children in the modeling and hint conditions. The predictor variables were age (older vs. younger toddlers), sex, prior knowledge (number of trials on which the child used a tool on the pretraining trials of Problem A), and whether the child was in the modeling condition or the hint condition. The dependent variable was the number of times (0–6)

TABLE 9

CORRELATION MATRIX OF VARIABLES INVOLVED IN THE COMPONENTIAL ANALYSES

	Condition	Age	Sex	Prior knowledge	Acquisition	Mapping	Strengthening	Refinement	Execution
Condition									
Age	.06								
Sex	.02	.05							
Prior knowledge	.14	.17	.34						
Acquisition	.33	.39	.13	.24					
Mapping	.11	.49	.19	.45	.62				
Strengthening	.04	.58	.32	.40	.64	.76			
Refinement	.25	.44	.27	.16	.46	.65	.72		
Execution	.15	.68	.29	.32	.52	.74	.81	.72	

Condition: Hint versus modeling

Age: 18–26 versus 27–35 months

Sex: Girl versus boy

Prior knowledge: Number of trials on which a tool was used on A1–3

Acquisition: Number of trials on which a tool was used on A4, A5, B4, and B5

Mapping: Number of trials on which a tool was used on B1 and C1

Strengthening: Number of trials on which a tool was used on B2, B3, C2, and C3

Refinement: Number of pretraining trials on which the target tool was used as first tool on B and C

Execution: Number of pretraining trials on which toy was obtained on B and C that each child obtained the toy on the pretraining trials of Problems B and C (the problems whose pretraining trials occurred after children had received instruction on prior problems).

Two distal variables accounted for 51% of the variance in the children's number of solutions on pretraining trials on Problems B and C. Age accounted for 45% of the variance and sex for an additional 6%. Older children solved more problems than did younger children, and boys solved more than girls.

The componential analysis allowed us to go beyond these distal predictors of performance to trace predictors of the paths of change shown by individual children. The initial analysis used the distal variables to predict the first component, acquisition of the tool strategy from instruction (i.e., number of posttraining trials, A4, A5, B4, and B5, on which a tool was used). Three variables accounted for 26% of the variance in whether children showed such initial acquisition. Age accounted for 13% of the variance, experimental condition accounted for an additional 8%, and prior knowledge accounted for an additional 5%. Older toddlers, toddlers in the modeling condition, and toddlers who used tools relatively often before instruction were more likely to use tools after instruction.

The next regression analysis examined mapping of learning from the original problem and context to new problems and contexts. Mapping was operationally defined as whether the child used the tool strategy on Trials B1 and C1. Performance on later pretraining trials would reflect within-problem learning as well as mapping, but performance on the initial trial on each problem would directly reflect mapping. The predictor variables were the same distal variables as in the previous analyses plus the measure of the prior component, acquisition. Three variables accounted for 52% of the variance in mapping. Acquisition accounted for 38% of the variance, prior knowledge for an additional 9%, and age for an additional 5%.

We next examined predictors of strengthening. Strengthening was measured by the number of tool uses on Trials B2, B3, C2, and C3. The independent variables were the same ones used as predictors of mapping, plus the measure of mapping itself. Four variables accounted for 69% of the variance in strengthening. As in the previous analysis, the preceding component, in this case mapping, was the best predictor of its immediate successor, in this case strengthening. Mapping accounted for 58% of the variance in strengthening. Age accounted for an additional 5% of variance (older children showed greater strengthening than would have been expected given their level of mapping), sex accounted for an additional 3% of variance (boys used the tools somewhat more than would have been expected from their level of mapping and age) and acquisition accounted for an additional 3%.

The next step was to examine predictors of refinement of choices. This dependent variable was measured in terms of number of pretraining trials on Problems B and C on which children chose the target tool as a means for obtaining the toy before they tried any other approach. The independent variables were the same as in the analysis of strengthening, plus the measure of strengthening itself. Two variables accounted for 55% of the variance in choice refinement. As in the last two analyses, the immediately preceding component was the best predictor of its successor. Strengthening accounted for 51% of the variance in choice refinement. The child's experimental group accounted for an additional 4% of the variance; children in the modeling condition more often chose the target tool first than children in the hint condition. As in previous analyses, it appeared that seeing the target tool used to obtain the toy helped the toddlers choose subsequent target tools.

The final step was to examine predictors of successful execution of the tool strategy. The dependent measure was the number of times toddlers obtained the toy on the pretraining trials of Problems B and C. The independent variables were all of those used to predict choice refinement, plus choice refinement itself. Three variables accounted for 74% of the variance. The best predictor of successful execution was the strengthening component. It accounted for 65% of the variance, somewhat more than the 53% accounted for by choice refinement. Age accounted for an additional 6% of variance, and choice refinement for an additional 3%.

Overall, the analysis of distal and proximal variables showed a clear pattern. Proficiency in the immediately preceding component usually was the best predictor of proficiency in the succeeding component. At the same time, distal variables exerted an influence above and beyond that of influencing the level of mastery of previous components. Particularly striking, age influenced three of the four "downstream" components, above and beyond the effects of the other variables. Older toddlers consistently did better on the later components than would have been expected from their status on the earlier components. Measuring both distal and proximal components thus allowed a more complete understanding of individual differences than could have been obtained by measuring either one alone.

AN ALTERNATIVE INTERPRETATION

The results suggested that toddlers in the modeling and hint conditions, especially older ones, relied predominantly on structural correspondences between target tools to map their learning from one problem to the next. Another interpretation also was plausible, however: Maybe the structurally similar target tool on the new problem looked more like the previous target tool to young children than did the tools that were decorated in the same way and were of the same color as the previous target. If this were the case, both structural and perceptual correspondences with the target tool on Problem A would have favored choice of the target tools on Problems B and C. Due to toddlers' limited verbal comprehension skills, we could not test this interpretation directly with them. We were able to test it, however, by conducting a separate experiment with preschoolers.

The participants were seventeen 5-year-olds. The materials were the tools and toys used in the main study with the toddlers. On each trial, we presented one of the target tools from the main experiment (e.g., the toy rake), all six tools from a different problem, and the toy that had been used with that set of six tools.

Children were asked to make both perceptual comparisons and functional comparisons. For the perceptual comparisons, the preschoolers were presented the target tool from one problem and all six tools from another. Then they were asked to select the item that "looks most like" the target tool. In the problem described earlier in this paragraph, they would be asked which of the six tools looked most like the toy rake.

For the functional comparisons, the experimenter first demonstrated how the previous target tool could be used to pull in a toy that was out of reach. The child was encouraged to imitate the action with the same tool. Then the experimenter presented the set of six tools from the other problem and asked the child to pick the tool that "can best do the same thing" as the tool they had seen.

Each child first was asked to make three perceptual comparisons and then three functional ones. The reason for asking them to make all of one type of comparison before any of the other was to avoid confusion about what was being asked on a particular question. The reason for always having children make the perceptual comparisons first was to avoid any possibility that focusing on the functional characteristics would bias their perceptual comparisons. The order of the three problems within each type of comparison was counterbalanced.

The results supported our original view regarding the relative similarity of the tools' perceptual appearances. Children literally never chose the new target tool as being the most perceptually similar to the previous target tool. In contrast, on 73% of trials (37 of 51), they chose the new target tool as the best for doing the same thing (pulling in the toy) as the previous target tool. Thus, in line with our expectation, the results of the main experiment reflected children having to choose whether to rely on perceptual similarity or on functional similarity, and for the most part relying on functional similarity to map what they had learned from one problem to another.

IX. HOW CHANGES OCCUR IN TODDLERS' THINKING

The purpose of this study was to start bridging the gap between the understanding of very early and later cognitive development. We pursued this goal by asking questions, using methods and measures, and generating representations of knowledge of toddlers' learning that correspond to those being used in contemporary process analyses of older children's learning. Overlapping waves theory, microgenetic methods, trial-by-trial strategy assessments, and a componential analysis that previously had proved useful for understanding learning and problem solving in older children all proved useful with toddlers as well. Thus, the study demonstrates that the gap can be bridged.

The microgenetic method used in this study provides a kind of microscope whose level of magnification can be turned up or down depending on the generality of the question being asked. Here, it allowed us to address both general and specific questions about toddlers' problem solving. At the most general level, results of the study conveyed a sense of the amount of learning and transfer that are possible for toddlers. Older toddlers in the modeling and hint conditions progressed from obtaining the toy on about 10% of pretraining trials on Problem A to obtaining it on almost 90% of pretraining trials on Problem C. At a more specific level, the results revealed the strategies used by 1.5- and 2.5-year-olds in their pursuit of the goal and how those strategies shifted over the course of the three problems. At a yet more specific level, the findings yielded information about the components that produced strategic change. The componential analysis allowed us to distinguish improvements that were due to increased use of the tool strategy from improvements due to increasingly refined choices among tools, and it allowed us to distinguish improvements due to each of these factors from improvements due to more skillful use of the target tool. The microgenetic method also provided information about change at different time grains for each level of analysis. It provided information about changes that occurred over the three problems, changes that occurred over trials within the same problem, and changes that occurred within individual trials.

This concluding part of this *Monograph* contains three sections. In this first section, we examine what the study tells us about toddlers' learning and problem solving. In the next section, we consider implications of the study for understanding cognitive development of older children. In the final section, we return to the initial phenomenon that inspired the study—the gap between our understanding of very young children's and older children's thinking and learning—and examine implications of the study for understanding of continuities and discontinuities between early and later learning processes.

DIMENSIONS OF COGNITIVE CHANGE

Cognitive change occurs along a number of dimensions. Five that are particularly important are the *path, rate, breadth, variability,* and *sources* of change. Subsets of these dimensions have been emphasized within developmental approaches emphasizing stages (e.g., Case, 1985; Flavell, 1971; Piaget, 1969), individual differences (e.g., Collins, 1991; McCall, Applebaum, & Hogarty, 1973), and learning (Brown, Bransford, Ferrara, & Campione, 1983; Klahr & MacWhinney, 1998). A comprehensive understanding of cognitive development, however, requires consideration of all of them. These dimensions have proved useful for describing cognitive change in older children (Siegler, 1995; Siegler & Stern, 1998). As indicated below, the dimensions are equally applicable for characterizing cognitive change in toddlers.

THE PATH OF CHANGE

A basic question regarding cognitive developmental change is whether children progress through qualitatively different understandings before reaching mature competence. This question has been highlighted in studies inspired by stage theories. As Flavell (1971) noted, a basic assumption of stage theories is that children progress through a sequence of qualitatively distinct understandings on their way to acquiring concepts and problem-solving skills.

The assumption of qualitative change is far from unique to stage theories. For example, privileged-domain approaches differ from stage theories in emphasizing the domain-specificity of cognitive growth. The two types of theories are similar, however, in positing that within each domain, children progress through qualitatively distinct knowledge states. Thus, Wellman (1990) proposed that children move from a very early desire theory of mind to a somewhat later belief-desire theory. Stage and privileged-domain approaches also are alike in their goal of describing *the* stage that children are in or *the* theory that they have. At a given point in time, children think in one way, and later they substitute a different, more advanced, way of thinking. Many information-processing approaches to development are similar in positing sequences of rules: young children use one rule, somewhat older children another, and so on (e.g., Klahr & Siegler, 1978).

The main traditional alternative to this perspective has been to portray cognitive development as involving continuous, quantitative growth. Psychometric theories, learning theories, connectionist theories, and growth curve modeling all take this approach (Bandura, 1977; Bayley, 1970; McClelland & Jenkins, 1991; Willett, 1997).

The present analysis of the development of toddlers' problem solving was based on a third perspective: that development involves a changing mix of ways of thinking. Qualitative change occurs, but it is qualitative change with a small q rather than a capital Q. That is, children often generate new ways of thinking, but the new ways of thinking are of limited range and scope. Most toddlers in the modeling and hint conditions of the present study experienced such qualitative change with a small q during the course of the experiment. Few of them knew the tool strategy at the outset, yet by the end, almost 90% were using tools.

Results of the present study also indicated important quantitative features of cognitive growth. With experience, children used the tool strategy increasingly consistently; they chose the optimal form of it increasingly often; and when they used it, they executed it increasingly well. Each of these quantitative changes contributed to their increasing success in obtaining the toy.

Comparing the idealized form of strategic development in Figure 1 with the data in Figure 7 shows that the toddlers' path of change on the toy-retrieval task adhered closely to the form envisioned within overlapping waves theory. At first, most children used either no strategy or the forward strategy; then the forward strategy became the most common, with the tool strategy also being used quite often; then the tool strategy became the most common approach, with the forward strategy remaining quite common. Throughout the experiment, children also continued to sometimes use no strategy or the indirect strategy. This strategic variability and wavelike pattern of change characterized individual children as well as the sample as a whole. On average, children used three strategies, and the large majority of children used either three or four approaches; only 3 of the 86 children always relied on a single approach.

Although individual children who showed substantial strategic change consistently followed the path depicted in Figure 7, whether children showed such change depended heavily on whether they received instruction. The path of change described in the previous paragraph was almost totally due to changes of children in the modeling and hint conditions. Children in the control condition showed a more meandering path of change, with little systematic change in strategy use over the three problems. Within the experimental groups, older toddlers made more dramatic switches toward use of the tool strategy, and toward consistent choice of the target tool, than did younger toddlers. The age difference was especially pronounced in the hint condition. Thus, experimental condition and age influenced the likelihood of children changing the strategies that they used, but it did not influence the path of change of those children who showed substantial change. This pattern of age and experimental condition influencing the probability of change, but of the path of change being quite similar across children in different conditions and of different ages, also has been observed with cognitive changes in older children (Alibali & Goldin-Meadow, 1993; Schauble, 1996).

One question that might be asked about this path of change was, "Why these strategies?" This question can be answered at two levels. One level emphasizes prior problem-solving experience and experience in the experimental situation. During infancy and the toddler period, children in the everyday environment frequently get desired objects by leaning forward and reaching for them, by asking their parents for help in obtaining them, and by looking at the desired objects and waiting for someone to help. In all likelihood, most infants and toddlers rarely if ever use tools to obtain toys that are out of reach. In the present experimental situation, however, the experimenter suggested to children that they might use the tools to obtain the toy. Those in the modeling and hint conditions were explicitly instructed in which tool to use and, in the modeling condition, were shown how to use it. Thus, everyday experiences and participation in the study provided a basis for children to use these four strategies.

But how did children know to try these strategies out of all the problem-solving approaches that they knew? The types of tools that they selected before they received any instruction suggest that they possessed some conceptual understanding of the requirements of the situation and the types of strategies that might succeed in it. On the first three trials of the experiment, toddlers already were biased toward choosing tools with shafts long enough to reach the toy and with a head that might be useful for raking it to them.

This selectivity suggests that the toddlers had the kind of goal sketch that Siegler and Crowley (1994) ascribed to older children in the context of arithmetic and that Bray, Fletcher, and Huffman (1999) ascribed to older children and adults in the context of memory strategies. The basic idea of a goal sketch is that people often have enough understanding of the goals that useful strategies in a domain must meet that they can rapidly devise plausible new strategies or choose from among their existing strategies ones that might be effective in a new situation. The toddlers' goal sketch for the toy-retrieval task seems likely to have included two main goals that strategies needed to meet: The strategy must allow them to make contact with the desired object (directly or indirectly), and the contact must be of a sort that could bring the desired object to them. Usually, the forward strategy would meet these goals, though in the present situation it did not; usually, asking one's parent for help, or looking imploringly toward the parent, also would be effective, though again in the present situation it was not; and usually, wielding a tool with a long enough shaft and a useful head would be effective, which in the present case it was.

Using no particular strategy might seem to present an exception to the general plausibility of toddlers' strategies for obtaining the toy. For toddlers, however, looking at a desired toy might quite often succeed in motivating someone to bring the toy to them. This last interpretation could be tested by presenting toddlers the tool-retrieval task without another person present, and determining whether reliance on just looking at the toy decreased.

In addition to the goal sketch hypothesis being in accord with the sensible strategies that the toddlers used, it also helps to explain the rapidity with which they learned the tool strategy from relevant instruction. Although most of the toddlers probably had not previously used a physical object to pull in a toy, seeing the model led almost all of them to learn to do so. And they learned quickly. On Trial A3, the trial immediately before the initial modeling, 10% of toddlers used a tool; on Trial A4, the trial immediately after modeling, 90% of them did. Clearly, the toddlers were well prepared to learn that tools could be effective for obtaining toys. It seems likely that conceptual understanding of the properties needed to bring objects to oneself facilitated this learning.

THE RATE OF CHANGE

The rapidity with which children came to rely consistently on the tool strategy varied greatly with their age and experimental condition. Older toddlers in both the modeling and hint conditions showed an immediate, large increase in tool use and problem solutions after receiving instruction on Problem A. They continued to use tools and to obtain the toy on most pretraining trials on Problem B. After training on Problem B, almost all of them used tools and obtained the toy, and almost as many did so on the pretraining trials of Problem C. Thus, the older toddlers showed quite rapid learning in both experimental conditions.

The younger toddlers showed more gradual change. Many in the hint condition never learned very well. Even on the posttraining trials of Problems A and B, fewer than 40% obtained the toy. The trend across the pretraining trials was gradually upward—from about 5% solutions on Problem A to around 20% on Problem B to around 35% on Problem C—but it was a slow process. The learning of younger toddlers in the modeling condition followed a different pattern, one with more dramatic ups and downs. They showed rapid initial learning after seeing the model; they progressed from less than 5% solutions on the pretraining trials of Problem A to more than 80% solutions on the posttraining trials of the problem. The learning proved to be specific to the problem on which they saw the modeling, however. When Problem B was presented, their performance dropped to the levels of their peers in the hint condition; both obtained the toy on only 15% to 20% of trials. After seeing the model demonstrate how Problem B could be solved, they once again succeeded on more than 80% of posttraining trials. This time, the learning proved more transferable; they succeeded in obtaining the toy on about 70% of pretraining trials on Problem C. Thus, the younger toddlers' learning was rapid on the specific problem on which they were trained, but it was more gradual across problems.

Instruction influenced the rate of learning in two distinct ways. The more straightforward way was that for older toddlers in both experimental conditions and for younger toddlers in the modeling condition, instruction led to much improved performance on the posttraining trials of the initial problem, and often to efforts to use the tool on the new problem as well. Beyond this, however, there also was improvement over the three pretraining trials of each problem, despite children not receiving any additional instruction during this period. Children in the control condition did not show comparable learning over the three pretraining trials. Thus, both the direct and indirect effects of modeling and verbal hints influenced the rate of learning.

THE BREADTH OF LEARNING

Learning a problem-solving skill in a particular context rarely does children much good. They also must be able to transfer the technique to other problems on which the same principles and solution strategies apply. Studies of adults' cognition and of older children's cognitive development have documented that learning often is more specific than seems optimal. Adults frequently learn to solve one problem but then fail when presented a second problem that has the identical structure and that can be solved in an identical way (Greeno, 1974; Simon & Hayes, 1976). Similarly, the fact that a 6-year-old knows how to solve number conservation problems is no guarantee that the child can solve liquid quantity and solid quantity conservation problems, despite the fact that the same logic can be applied to all three problems (Siegler, 1981). Moreover, schoolteachers at every level lament their students' failure to transfer what they have learned to new contexts (Glaser, 1982).

The present findings illustrated a complementary point that is often overlooked: Although learning may not be maximally general, it also is not maximally specific. This is true even when the learners are 1.5- and 2.5-year-olds. The large majority of toddlers who received modeling or hints learned to solve Problem A. They then were presented Problem B, which differed in the tools they needed to use; the toy that they were trying to obtain; the color, decoration, and form of the target tool; the type of table on which the toy and tool were placed; and, in two thirds of cases, whether they were presented the problems while sitting on their mother's lap or while standing in front of the table. Despite these many contextual differences, slightly more than half of the older toddlers in the modeling and hint conditions succeeded in solving the new problem from its very first presentation (Trial B1). Many of those who did not succeed at first were able to use the combination of the instruction and their new experience to figure out how to solve the problem by Trial B3. Thus, the differences between new and old problems reduced the number of children who obtained the toy, but most older toddlers still did. Younger toddlers' performance was disrupted to a greater extent by presentation of the first new problem, but in the modeling condition, most of them were able to succeed in obtaining the toy by the pretraining trials of Problem C.

One likely reason for the toddlers' relatively high amount of transfer is the goal sketch described in the previous section. The knowledge embodied in such a goal sketch would not only constrain in useful directions toddlers' initial attempts to obtain the toy and heighten their ability to learn from instruction in the original context, it also would help them transfer the learning to superficially different situations. The benefits of the goal sketch in promoting transfer seemed likely to take several forms. One would involve encoding; the goal sketch would lead children to encode the tools that were presented on new problems in terms of the length of their shafts and their type of head. Such encoding would help them choose the most promising tools on subsequent problems. Another benefit would involve the causal inferences toddlers would draw from the modeling, hints, and their own problem-solving experience. The toddlers would be biased toward relating the length of the shaft and the type of head on the trial to their, or the model's, success in obtaining the toy. In contrast, although the toddlers also might encode the target tool's color and decorative pattern, they would be biased against connecting these features to success in obtaining the toy. Thus, the toddlers' goal sketch seems likely to have constrained their initial performance, aided learning in its original context, and facilitated transfer.

Within the range of variation of problems in this study, the toddlers showed substantial transfer. Without question, however, they would show less transfer on tasks in which the solution principle applied in less obvious ways. This phenomenon is far from unique to toddlers' problem solving; it is equally pervasive in studies of infants' and toddlers' imitation (Barnat, Klein, & Meltzoff, 1996; Bauer & Dow, 1994) and in studies of older children's and adults' problem solving (DeLoache, Miller, & Pierroutsakos, 1998). Having a general understanding of the goals that must be met by successful strategies in a domain facilitates transfer, but it does not guarantee it. Generating useful procedures that reflect the understanding and executing the procedures effectively also are essential for meeting goals. Thus transferring knowledge to new contexts is a challenging problem for toddlers, as it is for learners of all ages (Bransford & Schwartz, in press; Brown, 1992).

THE VARIABILITY OF CHANGE

Longitudinal studies of individual differences have been the main technique used to examine the variability of change (Appelbaum & McCall, 1983; Nesselroade, 1990). The emphasis has been on stability of overall test performance or factor structure rather than on variation in specific cognitive processes. Such longitudinal analyses have provided a general depiction of the variability of cognitive change, but they have not provided much in-depth information on the variability of particular cognitive changes within and between children.

The present microgenetic study of toddlers' problem solving, like earlier microgenetic studies with older children and adults, indicated that substantial variability is present at every level of cognitive functioning. As discussed previously, the number of toddlers, particularly younger ones, who used the tool strategy following instruction on Problem A dropped considerably when Problem B was presented. Even after children began to use tools on a given problem, they quite often switched to a different strategy, usually the forward strategy, on a subsequent trial on that problem. Such switching occurred within individual trials as well; a child often started by using the forward strategy, and then switched to the tool strategy. Substantial variability was also present in children's choices of tools. Paralleling the choice of whether to use a tool at all, even children who previously had used the target tool often subsequently chose less effective tools. And even when children used the target tool, they used it with varying degrees of success. Executing the strategy effectively on a prior trial was no guarantee that they would execute it effectively on later ones. Thus, even after children had "acquired" the tool strategy, all of the other component processes of strategic change—mapping, strengthening, choice refinement, and execution—showed considerable variability.

The cognitive variability was especially great in the control condition, in the sense that almost all children in it continued to use a variety of strategies after they had begun to use the tool strategy. This more prolonged variability in the control condition was not surprising. Instruction can be viewed as having two main purposes: (a) teaching new approaches that people can use to solve problems, and (b) persuading people to stop using less effective previous approaches and instead to rely on the new approach. As Kuhn has noted (e.g., Kuhn, 1995; Kuhn, Amsel, & O'Laughlin, 1988), the latter goal often is often more difficult to achieve than the former. Older, less advantageous approaches frequently continue to be used long after superior new approaches are also known. In the present study, most toddlers in the control group started using the tool strategy at some point in the experiment, but it remained one among several approaches that they used. Toddlers in the modeling and hint conditions came to rely more consistently, though not exclusively, on the tool strategy. Thus, having the experimenter demonstrate the utility of the target tool or recommend it verbally decreased the variability of toddlers' strategies, above and beyond the effects of unguided experience in trying to obtain the toy. Similar findings have arisen with older children and adults in diverse contexts. In general, the more completely specified the instruction, the less variable the subsequent behavior (Joyce & Chase, 1990; Stokes & Balsam, 1999).

The microgenetic approach also yielded information about variability among individuals, that is, about individual differences. The traditional individual difference variables of age and sex both were related to toddlers' learning. Examining these distal variables, along with the proximal variables specified by the componential analysis, indicated how the distal variables exercised their effects. The componential analysis was especially revealing of the locus of sex differences. The fact that boys solved more problems than girls was due to their more often using the tool strategy, both before and after instruction. In contrast, when boys and girls used tools, they were comparably good at selecting the target tool from among the six possibilities, and they were comparably skillful at using the target tool to obtain the toy once they chose it. Put simply, boys were more likely than girls to use tools, both optimal and nonoptimal, but boys and girls were comparable in how well they chose among alternative tools and in how skillfully they used them.

Age exerted both direct effects on initial components in the causal chain and additional effects once degree of success on those earlier components was statistically taken into account. It not only was the best predictor of acquisition of the tool strategy; it also predicted mapping above and beyond the effect of acquisition, predicted strengthening above and beyond the effect of acquisition and mapping, and predicted successful execution, above and beyond the effect of acquisition, mapping, strengthening, and choice refinement. By contrast, sex accounted for additional variance only in the case of strengthening. This one unique effect of sex on a component process made sense, given that the locus of sex differences was the boys' greater eagerness to use the tools.

These analyses indicate that toddlers' problem solving exhibits all of the varied forms of variability that are evident in older children's problem solving. Variability involves more than some children performing better than others. It also includes variations in the strategies that children use, in how well they choose among different forms of a given strategy, and in how well they execute each strategy. Distinguishing conceptually among components of learning, and measuring them independently, can deepen our understanding of how traditional individual difference variables, such as age and sex, exert their influence on learning.

THE SOURCES OF CHANGE

We chose to examine the effects of modeling and verbal hints on toddlers' learning because these are two of the most common ways in which toddlers learn. Both instructional manipulations produced considerable learning, although with the younger toddlers, modeling was more effective than the verbal hint. Absolute majorities of older toddlers in both conditions and of younger toddlers in the modeling condition increased their use of the tool strategy and decreased their use of the forward strategy (and of using no strategy) over the three problems. In contrast, most younger toddlers in the hint condition continued to use the forward strategy on a high percentage of trials on all three problems, sometimes in conjunction with the tool strategy, sometimes not. The finding suggested that most younger toddlers needed the kind of concrete demonstration provided by the modeling in order to grasp the utility of the tool strategy, whereas older toddlers could grasp the tool strategy's utility just from verbal encouragement to try the target tool. This may be a quite general tendency; older toddlers may learn well from simply being told what to do, whereas younger toddlers may require showing as well as telling.

Modeling and verbal instruction have usually been discussed as social learning variables (e.g., Bandura, 1977; Grusec, 1988). The main goal of social learning research involving them has been to identify the conditions under which they exercise their effects, as opposed to getting inside the heads of children to identify the cognitive processes through which they operate. Thus, typical conclusions are that imitation is greater when models are powerful, when they are warm and responsive, and when they practice what they preach (Bandura, 1977; Yarrow, Scott, & Waxler, 1973).

There is no in-principle reason, however, not to consider the cognitive processes through which modeling and verbal instruction lead to changes in behavior. Indeed, in recent years, social learning theorists (e.g., Bandura, 1992) have placed increasing emphasis on cognitive processes. The level at which these theorists have analyzed the cognitive processes that influence social learning, however, is much less specific than the level at which cognitive process analyses are usually undertaken. The present study illustrates that relatively detailed analysis of the cognitive processes through which social learning occurs can also be fruitful, even with 1.5- and 2.5-year-olds.

The advantages of examining the effects of social learning variables at the level of specific cognitive processes can be seen by considering one of the most interesting changes in toddlers' problem solving that arose in this study: the improvement that toddlers in the modeling and hint conditions showed over the three pretraining trials of new problems. The differences between children in the experimental conditions and those in the control group grew considerably over these three trials, despite children in all three groups being treated identically on them. Thus, the positive effects of exposure to the modeling and hint continued to grow in the absence of further instruction. This within-problem improvement over the three pretraining trials was a pervasive phenomenon, seen on many measures: frequency of use of the tool strategy, percentage of choices of the target tool on trials on which a tool was used, successful execution of the tool strategy when children used a tool, and number of trials on which the toy was obtained.

The improvement occurred for the older toddlers from Trial B1 to B3, and for the younger toddlers in the modeling condition from Trial C1 to C3. Interestingly, the absolute point in learning at which the within-problem improvement began, and the height that it reached on that problem, were almost identical for the two groups that showed the improvement on Problem B and for the third group that showed it on Problem C. In all three cases, substantial within-problem improvement was seen when children reached a success rate of 50%–55% on the first trial of the new problem. In all three cases, success rates reached 75%–85% by the third trial of that problem (Figure 6). The consistency of the pattern suggested that on problems on which children require instruction to move beyond low levels of success, the instruction may have to lift their performance to a reasonably proficient level before they can learn from their own problem-solving efforts.

This pattern of learning, and the conditions that elicited it, are reminiscent of the type of cognitive scaffolding emphasized by cultural-contextualist theorists (Brown & Reeve, 1987; Bruner, 1983; Wood, 1989). Modeling and verbal hints helped structure the toy-retrieval task and indicated how goals could be attained. In the cases in which learning occurred over the pretraining trials, the instructional manipulations seem to have created a cognitive structure within which children could benefit from their own problem-solving efforts in the absence of further instruction.

How might modeling and verbal hints have created conditions under which toddlers could learn without additional instruction? Several processes probably contributed. The most obvious was that the instruction would have increased the likelihood of using the tool strategy, and of using the target tool, relative to alternative approaches. The ASCM model of strategy choice (Siegler & Shipley, 1995) illustrates how learning can occur through changing strengths of strategies. Strategy choice is a probabilistic process; the fact that a given strategy has been the most effective approach in the past does not mean that it will be consistently chosen in the future. Performance at the outset of the present study, the pretraining trials of Problem A, indicated that the tool strategy's strength was weak relative to competitors such as leaning forward and trying to grab the toy. Encountering the modeling or hint on Problem A, and subsequently obtaining the toy, would have strengthened the tendency to choose the target tool. On the pretraining trials of Problems B and C, when toddlers chose the target tool and obtained the toy, the strength of that approach would increase further, thus leading to increased tendencies to choose the target tool on subsequent trials. Strategies other than tool use never succeeded, and tools other than the target rarely did; trying them would reduce their future probability, thus making it more likely that children would choose the target tool on the next trial.

For this strengthening process to work effectively over trials, however, the strength of the target tool strategy already had to be reasonably high. If it was not, weakening another strategy would have little effect on the likelihood of the tool strategy being chosen (Siegler & Shipley, 1995). The similar operation of the simulation model provides a mechanistic account for why the improvement over trials did not occur until children's spontaneous likelihood of using the target tool was fairly high. Similar nonlinear effects of experience have arisen in connectionist models of cognitive development (e.g., McClelland, 1995) for basically the same reason.

A second process that probably gave rise to learning over the pretraining trials was opportunity for the toddlers to practice using the tools. Toddlers who used a tool on the new problem could improve their execution of the strategy. They might not succeed at first, either because they did not choose the target tool or because they used it clumsily, but they would be engaging in activities through which they could gain greater skill.

Encountering the model or the hint on earlier problem(s) also provided a resource for children to draw on if their initial attempts to solve a new problem failed. After such failure, they could search their memory for differences between what they did previously when they obtained the toy and what they did now when they failed to get it. This might lead them to recall, for example, that the tool they had used successfully had a head at a right angle to the shaft, whereas the tool they had just chosen did not. Children in the control group lacked such resources, because they had not succeeded earlier and thus lacked experiences of success that they could recall and analyze. This lack of success in obtaining the toy was probably why many toddlers in the control group used no strategy as late as Problem C, whereas almost no toddlers in the modeling or hint conditions did so.

A fourth way in which modeling and the hint may have contributed to children's ability to learn without further instruction was through its motivational effects. Having obtained the toy, they knew they could do it. Many children in the control condition never obtained the toy, and they may have become skeptical that it was even possible for them to do so.

All of these processes seem likely to amplify initial effects of instruction in a great many situations. Consider high school students who hear a lecture on some technique for solving algebra problems and who then solve a few problems using it. The instruction leads them to acquire the new technique at some level of strength. At first, the strength of the newly acquired strategy may be too low for the technique to be chosen consistently, especially on problems that look different from the ones on which the technique was learned. The experience of having used the technique successfully, however, would strengthen it to some degree, create a context in which the students could practice and become more skillful in using it, provide memory traces (and notes) that could be drawn upon if the technique failed in later applications, and bolster their confidence that they could succeed using it. Thus, although the phenomenon has not received much attention, self-generated learning that amplifies the effects of initial instruction seems likely to be pervasive across both tasks and age groups.

X. IMPLICATIONS FOR OLDER CHILDREN'S COGNITIVE DEVELOPMENT

Just as previous research on older children informed the present study of toddlers' thinking and learning, so the present study of toddlers can inform our understanding of thinking and learning in older children. In this section, we discuss implications of the present findings for understanding several areas of cognitive development in older children: analogical reasoning, utilization deficiencies, and learning.

ANALOGICAL REASONING

Most studies of preschoolers' and older children's analogical reasoning and problem solving have focused on demonstrating the importance of a single component of the overall process. For example, Inagaki and Hatano (1987) focused on initial acquisition of analogies; Gentner (e.g., Gentner & Medina, 1998; Kotovsky & Gentner, 1994) focused on the role of structure mapping, and Chen (1996) focused on execution of solution procedures.

In the present study, we examined the contributions of all of these component processes, as well as others such as choice refinement, to performance on a single analogical problem-solving task. All of the component processes proved to be important, in the sense that failure on any of them could short-circuit the problem-solving process. Some failures to obtain the toy were due to children not learning to use tools even on problems on which they received instruction. Others were due to children learning in the initial context but not mapping the tool strategy onto later, superficially different problems. Others were due to children using the tool strategy only sporadically. Yet others were due to children choosing an ineffective tool rather than the target. And some occurred when children chose the target tool but used it ineffectually.

Considering the whole range of components is essential for a comprehensive understanding not just of analogical problem solving at any one age but also of learning and development in this area. Both learning over the three problems and age-related differences in that learning included improvement in all five components. No one component would have accounted very well for either the effects of experience or the age-related differences in learning. The same seems likely to hold true for older children. This is critical for understanding the learning process: Failure to obtain one's goal is likely to interfere with learning, regardless of the source of the failure. If correct analogies do not allow the learner to achieve the desired goal, those analogies are unlikely to be strengthened as much as correct analogies that lead to goal attainment. Thus, comprehensive analyses of children's acquisition of analogical problem-solving skills will need to consider multiple components rather than focusing on a single process.

The present analysis also sheds light on a specific controversial issue within the analogical reasoning literature: the roles of superficial features and deep structure. Some investigators, such as Gentner (1989) and Tversky and Hemenway (1984), have argued that 3- to 6-year-olds rely primarily on superficial features and perceptual correspondence in drawing analogies, whereas older children rely primarily on deep structure and functional correspondence. Other investigators, such as Brown (1990), Goswami (1996), Kemler-Nelson (1995), and Kobayashi (1997), have argued that even 2- and 3-year-olds are not limited to drawing superficial analogies, that in domains that they understand, they rely primarily on structural correspondences.

The present findings were consistent with the latter position. The 1.5- and 2.5-year-olds in this study based choices primarily on structural correspondences between previous target tools and new potential tools. On the other hand, matches in superficial features between previous target tools and new tools also influenced the toddlers' choices. They more often chose suboptimal tools with colors and decorations that matched the previous target than otherwise identical tools with colors and decorations that did not match. This was especially true early in learning. Superficial similarities exercised a moderate effect on strategy choices on Problem B, but very little effect on choices on Problem C. Even on Problem B, however, deep structure similarities were more influential than were superficial ones. Thus, in domains in which toddlers understand the basic causal relations, their analogical reasoning, like that of older children, reflects influences of both deep structure and superficial features, though deep structure exercises a larger influence. The question is not "deep structure or superficial features," but rather when and how each type of resemblance influences analogical reasoning.

UTILIZATION DEFICIENCIES

The purpose of using a strategy is to attain a goal. Recent studies with preschoolers and older children, however, indicate that generating a new, relatively advanced strategy does not always help children achieve the goal that the strategy is intended to meet. The problem is that strategies that are useful in the long run are not always seen as useful in the short run. Sometimes, children derive no benefits in attaining goals from using new, potentially useful strategies. Other times, they benefit to a small degree, but not as much as they will once they have used the strategy more. Such "utilization deficiencies" (Miller, 1990) are quite common; they have been documented with diverse types of strategies, including attentional, memorial, and problem-solving strategies (for recent reviews of this literature, see Bjorklund, Miller, Coyle, & Slawinski, 1997, and Miller & Seier, 1994).

The microgenetic design and componential analysis used in the present study revealed several sources of utilization deficiencies, sources that probably contribute to utilization deficiencies in other contexts as well. One source was limited mapping. At first, the tool strategy was not applied as broadly as it could be. A second source of the early utilization deficiency involved the relatively low strength of the new strategy. Even in the context of the problem on which the tool strategy was acquired, it initially was not applied as consistently as it later was. A third source of utilization deficiencies was relatively unrefined choices among alternative versions of the tool strategy. Toddlers at first often chose tools that were not very useful; this led to their using the tool strategy but not obtaining the toy. Yet a fourth source was poor execution of the new strategy. Early in learning, even when toddlers chose the target tool, they fairly often failed to wield it sufficiently skillfully to meet their goal. As has been emphasized previously in this *Monograph*, acquiring a new strategy is only the beginning of strategic development. Mapping, strengthening, refinement of choices, and skillful execution all are needed before strategies reach their potential usefulness. Until that point, utilization deficiencies can be expected.

LEARNING

For many years, learning was *the* central topic in psychology in general and in developmental psychology in particular. With the cognitive revolution and the rise of Piaget, this hegemony was overthrown. Attention shifted from learning to thinking, an emphasis that has continued to this day. Even the term "learning" became perjorative, as in the phrase, "this is learning, not development." The movement away from studying learning was noted by a number of authorities in the 1983 edition of the *Handbook of Child Psychology*. In a particularly evocative description, Stevenson (1983) observed,

> As rapidly as the field (of learning) had developed, it went into decline. By the mid-1970s, articles on children's learning dwindled to a fraction of the number that had been published in the previous decade, and by 1980, it was necessary to search with diligence to uncover any articles at all. . . . The discussion of children's learning had been displaced by a newfound interest in cognitive development. (p. 213)

In a similar vein, Brown et al. (1983) noted, in their *Handbook* chapter, that although their title, "Learning, Remembering, and Understanding," included the term "learning," the research being reviewed focused almost exclusively on memory and comprehension.

The movement away from studying learning not only reflected a shift in interest; it also reflected an active skepticism about whether learning had much to do with development. Piaget went out of his way to distinguish between learning, by which he meant associative learning, and development, by which he meant the active construction of knowledge. This distinction was valuable in exposing hidden assumptions that had shaped earlier research on children's learning, but it had the unfortunate side effect of producing skepticism about the importance of any kind of learning for development. This skepticism was evident in the title of a volume edited by Liben (1987), *Development and Learning: Conflict or Congruence?* Asking whether learning and development were in conflict revealed an attitude that would have been unimaginable in an earlier era.

Stevenson (1983), Brown et al. (1983), and a number of contemporaries who noted the movement away from studying children's learning (e.g., Case, 1985) predicted that the area would make a comeback. All gave the same reason: the inherent importance of the topic. Their prediction proved prophetic—to a degree. There indeed has been increasing interest in children's learning, but the trend would more accurately be characterized as a boomlet than as a boom. The interest also has been more evident in increased theorizing about children's learning (e.g., Gelman & Williams, 1998; Keil, 1998; Thelen & Smith, 1998; Wellman & Gelman, 1998) than in empirical studies that examine learning as it occurs. Studies of preschoolers' and older children's learning have started to appear in greater numbers, but the quantity of such studies remains a small fraction of the number of studies on such specific topics as infants' object permanence, preschoolers' theory of mind, and preschoolers' and older children's eyewitness testimony. And, as noted above, the number of studies that focus on infants' and toddlers' learning of cognitive capabilities is even smaller than the number that focus on older children's learning of them.

There are numerous reasons for the paucity of empirical studies of children's learning. It makes sense to determine what children know at different ages before trying to determine how they get from here to there. Examining what children know at any one time is easier than assessing initial knowledge and then going on to examine how they build on that base to acquire new knowledge. The great recent progress in understanding the topics that have been in vogue, such as theory of mind, has created its own momentum, raising numerous interesting questions regarding alternative interpretations and potential extensions of previous findings.

Arrayed against these varied reasons that militate in favor of continuing to focus on children's knowledge, rather than on their learning, is one central fact: Learning is omnipresent in children's lives. Brown and DeLoache (1978) aptly characterized young children as "universal novices." The only way in which they can acquire greater expertise is through learning. Knowing what children's thinking is like at different ages, without knowing how they get from here to there, is an inherently unsatisfying state of affairs.

A major purpose of the present study was to illustrate that we can move beyond this unsatisfying state. Very young children's learning, like older children's learning, can be studied in ways that yield rich and revealing data, data that broaden our understanding of developmental differences, individual differences, and a variety of other topics.

In addition to yielding interesting data about an omnipresent aspect of children's lives, studies of learning have an additional advantage: They can help unify our understanding of cognitive development. A number of recent reviewers have lamented the fragmentation of the field of cognitive development into a number of small, specialized subareas without unifying theories or frameworks (e.g., Case, 1998; DeLoache, Miller, & Pierroutsakos, 1998; Haith & Benson, 1998). The deemphasis of learning may have a great deal to do with this. When learning theory was ascendant, the stated goal was to identify universal "laws of learning" that would apply across ages, species, and conditions. This proved to be a dead end; learning is influenced by the kind of organism doing the learning, the content being learned, and the conditions under which learning occurs.

Newer theories of learning recognize the importance of considering the learner's species and developmental status, as well as the content being learned and the context within which the learning is occurring. These newer theories, however, also are beginning to identify similarities in learning processes across these variables. In one notable example, Gelman and Williams (1998) highlighted the importance of constraints for facilitating learning in all types of domains, both biologically privileged and nonprivileged. Similarly, Keil (1989, 1998) and Wellman and Gelman (1998) emphasized formation of theories that stress causal linkages as a crucial part of children's learning in a broad range of domains. Thelen and Smith (1998) and Bertenthal and Clifton (1998) focused on the importance of considering the physical situation; the learner's anatomical properties, coordination, and learning history inside and outside of the current situation; and numerous other influences for understanding acquisition of cognition, perception, and action. In yet another example, Siegler (1989) noted that the best-specified models of children's learning all shared the same structure, a structure within which learning consisted of mechanisms for generating variation, mechanisms for selecting among the variants, and mechanisms by which the more successful variants became increasingly common.

The present observations of toddlers' learning provided evidence supporting all of these theoretical perspectives on learning. Toddlers' choices among tools were constrained in useful ways even before they received any instruction on the task. They predominantly chose tools with shafts long enough to reach the toy and with a head that could be useful for pulling it in. This tendency to choose tools from the outset that had the right causal properties, together with the rapidity with which children benefited from the modeling and hint, suggested that they were attending to causal relations between properties of the tools and requirements for obtaining the toy. Success in obtaining the toy depended not just on acquiring the tool strategy but on the toddlers' motoric skill and coordination, base-rate of using tools to try to obtain the toy, previous exposure to modeling or hints, and a host of other influences. The toddlers generated a variety of strategies, they tended to choose the most useful strategy, and they preserved the lessons of past experience in mapping their learning onto novel problems.

The present results also illustrated a number of other cross-domain and cross-age similarities in learning processes. The 1.5- and 2.5-year-olds' learning about tools reflected the same component processes as 5-year-olds' learning about conservation and 8-year-olds' acquisition of an arithmetic insight (Siegler, 1995; Siegler & Stern, 1998). Strategic change involved improvement in all five components, rather than just substitution of a more advanced strategy for a less advanced one. Although amount of learning varied with the learner's age, sex, and initial knowledge, the components of learning were the same for older and younger toddlers, boys and girls, and children with greater and lesser initial knowledge.

In general, the process of learning may share more commonalities across ages, domains, and tasks than the products of learning. What children know at a given time inevitably reflects the amount of experience that they have had in the domain, the rate at which they learned from their experiences, the difficulty of the material being learned, the conditions under which learning occurred, and many other variables. The processes through which children learn, however, may share many commonalities that hold over diverse types of learners, material being learned, and learning contexts. If this is the case, focusing on the processes through which children learn may help unify the fragmented field of cognitive development.

XI: CONCLUSIONS: BRIDGING THE GAP

The main goal of this study has been to bridge the gap between research on very early and later cognitive development. Research on infants' and toddlers' cognition has differed from research on the cognition of older children in the questions that have been asked, the methods and measures that have been used, and the way that knowledge has been represented. In the present study, we applied the overlapping waves theory and the microgenetic method, which had been developed in the context of older children's cognitive development, to examining toddlers' problem solving and learning. Not only did the general theory and methodology prove applicable to this much younger population, but a specific componential analysis, developed to account for older children's learning of scientific and mathematical concepts, also proved useful for characterizing how toddlers learn to use tools to obtain toys that are out of reach.

Many specific results also were similar. Like older children, the toddlers used several problem-solving strategies from the beginning of learning; they continued to use less advantageous strategies even after they learned a more advantageous one; they chose among strategies in fairly adaptive ways from the beginning of learning; their choices became increasingly adaptive with problem-solving experience; their mapping of what they had learned to novel problems was influenced primarily by structural similarities; superficial similarities also exerted some influence on their choices; they switched strategies not only from problem to problem but also from trial to trial within a problem; they fairly often switched strategies within a single trial; and improved execution was necessary for the optimal strategy to consistently allow them to achieve their goal.

A more general similarity also was present: Toddlers, like older children, emerged as active thinkers and learners. This was perhaps most evident in their success in learning from their own problem-solving experience. Children who had received the modeling or verbal hint showed a certain amount of direct transfer when they encountered a novel problem. They went on, however, to learn from their efforts to solve the novel problem, so that their performance continued to improve without further instruction. Children in the control group did not show comparable learning over these trials. Thus, children learned through integrating earlier instruction with subsequent problem-solving experience.

This integration of instruction with the lessons of one's own experience is not what would be expected if toddlers were passive learners. But, of course, they are not. Studying children's learning in no way requires that we buy into the assumptions of the learning theories of the 1950s and 1960s. It does demand, however, that we recognize that the only way to understand development as a process is to study learning while it is occurring.

REFERENCES

Acredolo, C., O'Conner, J., & Horobin, K. (1989, March). *Children's understanding of conservation: From possibility to probability to necessity.* Poster session presented at the biennial meeting of the Society for Research in Child Development, Kansas City, MO.

Adolph, K. E. (1997). Learning in the development of infant locomotion. *Monographs of the Society for Research in Child Development, 62* (3, Serial No. 251).

Alibali, M. W. (1999). How children change their minds: Strategy change can be gradual or abrupt. *Developmental Psychology, 35,* 127–145.

Alibali, M. W., & Goldin-Meadow, S. (1993). Gesture-speech mismatch and mechanisms of learning: What the hands reveal about a child's state of mind. *Cognitive Psychology, 25,* 468–573.

Amsel, E., Goodman, G., Savoie, D., & Clark, M. (1996). The development of reasoning about causal and non-causal influences on levers. *Child Development, 67,* 1624–1646.

Anderson, J. R. (1991). Is human cognition adaptive? *The Behavioral and Brain Sciences, 14,* 471–484.

Anglin, J. M. (1993). Vocabulary development: A morphological analysis. *Monographs of the Society for Research in Child Development, 58* (10, Serial No. 238).

Appelbaum, M. I., & McCall, R. B. (1983). Design and analysis in developmental psychology. In P. H. Mussen (Series Ed.) & W. Kessen (Vol. Ed.), *Handbook of child psychology: Vol. 1. History, theory and methods.* New York: Wiley.

Baillargeon, R. (1987). Object permanence in 3 1/2- and 4 1/2-month-old infants. *Developmental Psychology, 23,* 655–664.

Bandura, A. (1977). *Social learning theory.* Englewood Cliffs, NJ: Prentice-Hall.

Bandura, A. (1992). Perceived self-efficacy in cognitive development and functioning. *Educational Psychologist, 28,* 117–148.

Barnat, B. B., Klein, P. J., & Meltzoff, A. N. (1996). Deferred imitation across changes in context and object: Memory and generalization in 14-month-old infants. *Infant Behavior and Development, 19,* 241–252.

Bauer, P. J., & Dow, G. A. (1994). Episodic memory in 16- and 20-month-old children: Specifics are generalized but not forgotten. *Developmental Psychology, 30,* 403–417.

Bauer, P. J., & Mandler, J. M. (1992). Putting the horse before the cart: The use of temporal order in recall of events by one-year-old children. *Developmental Psychology, 28,* 441–452.

Bayley, N. (1970). Development of mental abilities. In P. H. Mussen (Ed.), *Carmichael's manual of child psychology* (3rd ed., Vol. 1). New York: Wiley.

Bertenthal, B. I., & Clifton, R. K. (1998). Perception and action. In W. Damon (Series Ed.) & D. Kuhn & R. S. Siegler (Vol. Eds.), *Handbook of child psychology: Vol. 2. Cognition, perception & language* (5th ed.). New York: Wiley.

Bjorklund, D. F., & Coyle, T. R. (1995). Utilization deficiencies in the development of memory strategies. In F. E. Weinert & W. Schneider (Eds.), *Memory performance and competencies: Issues in growth and development*. Hillsdale, NJ: Erlbaum.

Bjorklund, D. F., Coyle, T. R., & Gaultney, J. F. (1992). Developmental differences in the acquisition and maintenance of an organizational strategy: Evidence for utilization deficiency hypothesis. *Journal of Experimental Child Psychology*, **54**, 434–438.

Bjorklund, D. F., Miller, P. H., Coyle, T. R., & Slawinski, J. L. (1997). Instructing children to use memory strategies: Evidence of utilization deficiencies in memory training studies. *Developmental Review*, **17**, 411–441.

Bransford, J. D., & Schwartz, D. L. (in press). Rethinking transfer: A simple proposal with education implications. In A. Iran-Nejad & P. D. Pearson (Eds.), *Review of research in education* (Vol. 24). Washington, DC: American Educational Research Association.

Bray, N. W., Fletcher, L. F., & Huffman, K. L. (1999). Developmental and intellectual differences in self-report and strategy use. *Developmental Psychology*, **35**, 1223–1236.

Brown, A. L. (1990). Domain-specific principles affect learning and transfer in children. *Cognitive Science*, **14**, 107–133.

Brown, A. L. (1992). Design experiments: Theoretical and methodological challenges in creating complex interventions in classroom settings. *The Journal of the Learning Sciences*, **2**, 141–178.

Brown, A. L., Bransford, J. D., Ferrara, R. A., & Campione, J. C. (1983). Learning, remembering, and understanding. In P. H. Mussen (Series Ed.) & J. H. Flavell & E. M. Markman (Vol. Eds.), *Handbook of child psychology: Vol. 3. Cognitive development*. New York: Wiley.

Brown, A. L., & DeLoache, J. (1978). Skills, plans, and self-regulation. In R. S. Siegler (Ed.), *Children's thinking: What develops?* Hillsdale, NJ: Erlbaum.

Brown, A. L., & Reeve, R. A. (1987). Bandwidths of competence: The role of supportive contexts in learning and development. In L. S. Liben (Ed.), *Development and learning: Conflict or congruence*. Hillsdale, NJ: Erlbaum.

Brown, J. S., & Burton, R. B. (1978). Diagnostic models for procedural bugs in basic mathematical skills. *Cognitive Science*, **2**, 155–192.

Bruner, J. S. (1983). *Child's talk: Learning to use language*. New York: Norton.

Case, R. (1985). *Intellectual development: A systematic reinterpretation*. New York: Academic Press.

Case, R. (1998). The development of conceptual structures. In W. Damon (Series Ed.) & D. Kuhn & R. S. Siegler (Vol. Eds.), *Handbook of child psychology: Vol. 2. Cognition, perception & language* (5th ed.). New York: Wiley.

Chen, Z. (1996). Children's analogical problem solving: The effects of superficial, structural, and procedural similarity. *Journal of Experimental Child Psychology*, **62**, 410–431.

Chen, Z., & Klahr, D. (1999). All other things being equal: Children's acquisition of the Control of Variables Strategy. *Child Development*, **70**, 1098–1120.

Chen, Z., Sanchez, R. P., & Campbell, T. (1997). From beyond to within their grasp: The rudiments of analogical problem solving in 10- and 13-month-olds. *Developmental Psychology*, **33**, 790–801.

Church, R. B., & Goldin-Meadow, S. (1986). The mismatch between gesture and speech as an index of transitional knowledge. *Cognition*, **23**, 43–71.

Clifton, R. K., Muir, D. W., Ashmead, D. H., & Clarkson, M. G. (1993). Is visually guided reaching in early infancy a myth? *Child Development*, **64**, 1099–1110.

Collins, L. M. (1991). Measurement in longitudinal research. In L. M. Collins & J. L. Horn (Eds.), *Best methods for the analysis of change: Recent advances, unanswered questions, future directions*. Washington, DC: American Psychological Association.

Coyle, T. R., & Bjorklund, D. F. (1997). Age differences in, and consequences of, multiple- and variable-strategy use on a multitrial sort-recall task. *Developmental Psychology,* **33**, 372–380.

Crowley, K., & Siegler, R. S. (1999). Explanation and generalization in young children's strategy learning. *Child Development,* **70**, 304–317.

DeLoache, J. S. (1995). Early symbol understanding and use. In *The Psychology of Learning and Motivation.* New York: Academic Press.

DeLoache, J. S., Miller, K. F., & Pierroutsakos, S. L. (1998). Reasoning and problem solving. In W. Damon (Series Ed.) & D. Kuhn & R. S. Siegler (Vol. Eds.), *Handbook of child psychology: Vol. 2. Cognition, perception & language* (5th ed.). New York: Wiley.

Flavell, J. H. (1971). Stage-related properties of cognitive development. *Cognitive Psychology,* **2**, 421–453.

Flavell, J. H. (1984). Discussion. In R. J. Sternberg (Ed.), *Mechanisms of cognitive development.* New York: Freeman.

Gelman, R., & Williams, E. (1998). Enabling constraints for cognitive development and learning: Domain specificity and epigenesis. In W. Damon (Series Ed.) & D. Kuhn & R. S. Siegler (Vol. Eds.), *Handbook of child psychology: Vol. 2. Cognition, perception & language* (5th ed.). New York: Wiley.

Gentner, D. (1989). The mechanisms of analogical transfer. In S. Vosniadou & A. Ortony (Eds.), *Similarity and analogical reasoning.* London: Cambridge University Press.

Gentner, D., & Medina, J. (1998). Similarity and the development of rules. *Cognition,* **65**, 263–297.

Glaser, R. (Ed.). (1982). *Advances in instructional psychology.* Hillsdale, NJ: Erlbaum.

Goldin-Meadow, S., Alibali, M. W., & Church, R. B. (1993). Transitions in concept acquisition: Using the hand to read the mind. *Psychological Review,* **100**, 279–297.

Goodall, J. (1986). *The chimpanzees of Gombe: Patterns of behavior.* Cambridge, MA: Harvard University Press.

Goswami, U. (1996). Analogical reasoning and cognitive development. In H. Reese (Ed.), *Advances in child development and behavior* (Vol. 26). New York: Academic Press.

Graham, T., & Perry, M. (1993). Indexing transitional knowledge. *Developmental Psychology,* **29**, 779–788.

Granott, N. (1993). Patterns of interaction in the co-construction of knowledge: Separate minds, joint effort, and weird creatures. In R. Wozniak & K. W. Fischer (Eds.), *Development in context: Acting and thinking in specific environments.* Hillsdale, NJ: Erlbaum.

Granott, N. (1998). A paradigm shift in the study of development: Essay review of *Emerging Minds* by R. S. Siegler. *Human Development,* **41**, 360–365.

Greeno, J. G. (1974). Hobbits and orcs: Acquisition of a sequential concept. *Cognitive Psychology,* **6**, 270–292.

Grusec, J. E. (1988). *Social development: History, theory, and research.* New York: Springer-Verlag.

Haith, M. M. (1993). Future-oriented processes in infancy: The case of visual expectations. In C. E. Granrud (Ed.), *Visual perception and cognition in infancy.* Hillsdale, NJ: Erlbaum.

Haith, M. M., & Benson, J. (1998). Infant cognition. In W. Damon (Series Ed.) & D. Kuhn & R. S. Siegler (Vol. Eds.), *Handbook of child psychology: Vol. 2. Cognition, perception & language* (5th ed.). New York: Wiley.

Hofsten, C. von, Spelke, E., Feng, Q., & Vishton, P. (1994, June). *Predictive reaching for poorly occluded objects.* Paper presented at the Nineteenth Biennial International Conference for Infant Studies, Paris, France.

Horowitz, F. D. (1995). The challenge facing infant research in the next decade. In G. J. Suci & S. S. Robertson (Eds.), *Future directions in infant development research.* New York: Springer-Verlag.

Inagaki, K., and Hatano, G. (1987). Young children's spontaneous personification as analogy. *Child Development*, **58**, 1013–1020.

Inhelder, B., Ackerman-Vallado, E., Blanchet, A., Karmiloff-Smith, A., Kilcher-Hagedorn, H., Montagero, J., & Robert, M. (1976). The process of invention in cognitive development: A report of research in progress. *Archives de Psychologie*, **171**, 57–72.

Johnson, K. E., & Mervis, C. B. (1994). Microgenetic analysis of first steps in children's acquisition of expertise on shorebirds. *Developmental Psychology*, **30**, 418–435.

Joyce, J. H., & Chase, P. N. (1990). Effects of response variability on the sensitivity of rule-governed behavior. *Journal of the Experimental Analysis of Behavior*, **54**, 251–262.

Karmiloff-Smith, A. (1979). Micro- and macro-developmental changes in language acquisition and other representational systems. *Cognitive Science*, **3**, 91–118.

Karmiloff-Smith, A. (1984). Children's problem solving. In M. Lamb, A. L. Brown, & B. Rogoff (Eds.), *Advances in developmental psychology* (Vol. 3). Hillsdale, NJ: Erlbaum.

Karmiloff-Smith, A. (1986). Stage/structure versus phase/process in modelling linguistic and cognitive development. In I. Levin (Ed.), *Stage and structure: Reopening the debate*. Norwood, NJ: Ablex.

Karmiloff-Smith, A. (1992). *Beyond modularity: A developmental perspective on cognitive science*. Cambridge, MA: MIT Press.

Keil, F. C. (1989). *Concepts, kinds, and cognitive development*. Cambridge, MA: Bradford Books/MIT Press.

Keil, F. C. (1998). Cognitive science and the origins of thought and knowledge. In W. Damon (Series Ed.) & R. M. Lerner (Vol. Ed.), *Handbook of child psychology: Vol. 1. Theoretical models of human development* (5th ed.). New York: Wiley.

Kemler-Nelson, D. G. (1995). Principle-based inferences in young children's categorization: Revisiting the impact of function in the naming of artifacts. *Cognitive Development*, **10**, 347–380.

Klahr, D., & MacWhinney, B. (1998). Information processing. In W. Damon (Series Ed.) & D. Kuhn & R. S. Siegler (Vol. Eds.), *Handbook of child psychology: Vol. 2. Cognition, perception & language* (5th ed.). New York: Wiley.

Klahr, D., & Siegler, R. S. (1978). The representation of children's knowledge. In H. Reese & L. Lipsitt (Eds.), *Advances in child development and behavior.* (Vol. 12). New York: Academic Press.

Kobayashi, H. (1997). The role of actions in making inferences about the shape and material of solid objects among Japanese 2 year-old children. *Cognition*, **63**, 251–269.

Kohler, W. (1925). *The mentality of apes.* New York: Liveright.

Kotovsky, L., & Gentner, D. (1994). Comparison and categorization in the development of relational similarity. *Child Development*, **67**, 2797–2822.

Kuhn, D. (1995). Microgenetic study of change: What has it told us? *Psychological Science*, **6**, 133–139.

Kuhn, D., Amsel, E., & O'Laughlin, M. (1988). *The development of scientific thinking skills.* San Diego, CA: Academic Press.

Kuhn, D., Garcia-Mila, M., Zohar, A., & Andersen, C. (1995). Strategies of knowledge acquisition. *Monographs of the Society for Research in Child Development*, **60** (4, Serial No. 245).

Lemaire, P., & Siegler, R. S. (1995). Four aspects of strategic change: Contributions to children's learning of multiplication. *Journal of Experimental Psychology: General*, **124**, 83–97.

Leslie, A. M. (1982). The perception of causality in infants. *Perception*, **11**, 173–186.

Liben, L. S. (Ed.) (1987). *Development and learning: Conflict or congruence*. Hillsdale, NJ: Erlbaum.

McCall, R. B., Appelbaum, M. I., & Hogarty, P. S. (1973). Developmental changes in mental performance. *Monographs of the Society for Research in Child Development*, **38** (3, Serial No. 150).

McCarty, M. E., Clifton, R. K., & Collard, R. R. (1999). Problem solving in infancy: The emergence of an action plan. *Developmental Psychology*, **35**, 1091–1101.

McClelland, J. L. (1995). A connectionist perspective on knowledge and development. In T. J. Simon & G. S. Halford (Eds.), *Developing cognitive competence: New approaches to process modeling*. Hillsdale, NJ: Erlbaum.

McClelland, J., & Jenkins, E. (1991). Nature, nurture, and connections: Implications of connectionist models for cognitive development. In K. van Lehn (Ed.), *Architectures for intelligence*. Hillsdale, NJ: Erlbaum.

McGilly, K., & Siegler, R. S. (1990). The influence of encoding and strategic knowledge on children's choices among serial recall strategies. *Developmental Psychology*, **26**, 931–941.

Meltzoff, A. N. (1988). Infant imitation and memory: Nine-month olds in immediate and deferred tests. *Child Development*, **59**, 217–225.

Meltzoff, A. N., & Moore, M. K. (1998). Object representation, identity, and the paradox of early permanence: Steps toward a new framework. *Infant Behavior & Development*, **21**, 201–235.

Metz, K. (1985). The development of children's problem solving in a gears task: A problem space perspective. *Cognitive Science*, **9**, 431–472.

Metz, K. E. (1998). Emergent understanding and attribution of randomness: Comparative analysis of the reasoning of primary grade children and undergraduates. *Cognition and Instruction*, **16**, 285–365.

Miller, P. H. (1990). The development of strategies of selective attention. In D. F. Bjorklund (Ed.), *Children's strategies: Contemporary views of cognitive development*. Hillsdale, NJ: Erlbaum.

Miller, P., & Aloise-Young, P. (1996). Preschoolers' strategic behaviors and performance on a same-different task. *Journal of Experimental Child Psychology*, **60**, 284–303.

Miller, P. H., & Coyle, T. R. (1999). Developmental change: Lessons from microgenesis.

Miller, P. H., & Seier, W. L. (1994). Strategy utilization deficiencies in children: When, where, and why. In H. W. Reese (Ed.), *Advances in child development and behavior* (Vol. 25). New York: Academic Press.

Mosier, C. E., & Rogoff, B. (1994). Infants' instrumental use of their mothers to achieve their goals. *Child Development*, **65**, 70–79.

Nesselroade, J. R. (1990). The warp and the woof of the developmental fabric. In R. Downs, L. Liben, & D. S. Palermo (Eds.), *Visions of development, the environment, and aesthetics: The legacy of Joachim F. Wohlwill*. Hillsdale, NJ: Lawrence Erlbaum.

Neuringer, A. (1993). Reinforced variation and selection. *Animal Learning & Behavior*, **21**, 83–91.

Newell, A., & Simon, H. A. (1972). *Human problem solving*. Englewood Cliffs, NJ: Prentice-Hall.

Oakes, L. M. (1994). The development of infants' use of continuity cues in their perception of causality. *Developmental Psychology*, **30**, 869–879.

Oakes, L. M., & Cohen, L. B. (1995). Infant causal perception. In C. Rovee-Collier & L. P. Lipsitt (Eds.), *Advances in infancy research*. (Vol. 9). Norwood, NJ: Ablex.

Piaget, J. (1969). *The child's conception of physical causality*. Totowa, NJ: Littlefield, Adams, & Co.

Piaget, J. (1971). *The construction of reality in the child*. New York: Ballantine.

Rittle-Johnson, B. R. (1999). *The development of conceptual and procedural knowledge of mathematics: A microgenetic analysis*. Unpublished doctoral dissertation, Carnegie Mellon University, Pittsburgh, PA.

Rittle-Johnson, B. R., & Siegler, R. S. (1999). Learning to spell: Variability, choice, and change in children's strategy use. *Child Development*, **70**, 332–348.

Russell, J. (1996). *Agency: Its role in mental development.* Hove, East Sussex, England: Erlbaum/ Taylor & Francis.

Schauble, L. (1990). Belief revision in children: The role of prior knowledge and strategies for generating evidence. *Journal of Experimental Child Psychology*, **49**, 31–57.

Schauble, L. (1996). The development of scientific reasoning in knowledge-rich contexts. *Developmental Psychology*, **32**, 102–119.

Schneider, W., Korkel, J., & Weinert, F. E. (1989). Domain-specific knowledge and memory performance: A comparison of high- and low-aptitude children. *Journal of Educational Psychology*, **81**, 306–312.

Shrager, J., & Siegler, R. S. (1998). SCADS: A model of children's strategy choices and strategy discoveries. *Psychological Science*, **9**, 405–410.

Siegler, R. S. (1981). Developmental sequences within and between concepts. *Monographs of the Society for Research in Child Development*, **46** (2, Serial No. 189).

Siegler, R. S. (1987). The perils of averaging data over strategies: An example from children's addition. *Journal of Experimental Psychology: General*, **116**, 250–264.

Siegler, R. S. (1988). Strategy choice procedures and the development of multiplication skill. *Journal of Experimental Psychology: General*, **117**, 258–275.

Siegler, R. S. (1989). Mechanisms of cognitive development. *Annual Review of Psychology*, **40**, 353–379.

Siegler, R. S. (1994). Cognitive variability: A key to understanding cognitive development. *Current Directions in Psychological Science*, **3**, 1–5.

Siegler, R. S. (1995). How does change occur: A microgenetic study of number conservation. *Cognitive Psychology*, **28**, 225–273.

Siegler, R. S. (1996). *Emerging minds: The process of change in children's thinking.* New York: Oxford University Press.

Siegler, R. S., & Chen, Z. (1998). Developmental differences in rule learning: A microgenetic analysis. *Cognitive Psychology*, **36**, 273–310.

Siegler, R. S., & Crowley, K. (1991). The microgenetic method: A direct means for studying cognitive development. *American Psychologist*, **46**, 606–620.

Siegler, R. S., & Crowley, K. (1994). Constraints on learning in non-privileged domains. *Cognitive Psychology*, **27**, 194–227.

Siegler, R. S., & Jenkins, E. A. (1989). *How children discover new strategies.* Hillsdale, NJ: Erlbaum.

Siegler, R. S., & Lemaire, P. (1997). Older and younger adults' strategy choices in multiplication: Testing predictions of ASCM via the choice/no-choice method. *Journal of Experimental Psychology: General*, **126**, 71–92.

Siegler, R. S., & McGilly, K. (1989). Strategy choices in children's time-telling. In I. Levin and D. Zakay (Eds.), *Time and human cognition: A life span perspective.* The Netherlands: Elsevier Science Publishers.

Siegler, R. S., & Shipley, C. (1995). Variation, selection, and cognitive change. In T. Simon and G. Halford (Eds.), *Developing cognitive competence: New approaches to process modeling.* Hillsdale, NJ: Erlbaum.

Siegler, R. S., & Stern, E. (1998). A microgenetic analysis of conscious and unconscious strategy discoveries. *Journal of Experimental Psychology: General*, **127**, 377–397.

Simon, H. A., & Hayes, J. R. (1976). The understanding process: Problem isomorphs. *Cognitive Psychology*, **8**, 165–190.

Staszewski, J. J. (1988). Skilled memory and expert mental calculation. In M. T. H. Chi, R. Glaser, & M. J. Farr (Eds.), *The nature of expertise.* Hillsdale, NJ: Erlbaum.

Sternberg, R. J. (1985). *Beyond IQ: A triarchic theory of human intelligence.* New York: Cambridge University Press.

Stevenson, H. (1983). How children learn: The quest for a theory. In P. H. Mussen (Series Ed.) & W. Kessen (Vol. Ed.), *Handbook of child psychology: Vol. 1. History, theory and methods.* New York: Wiley.

Stokes, P. D. (1995). Learned variability. *Animal Learning & Behavior, 23,* 164–176.

Stokes, P. D., & Balsam, P. (1999). *A critical period for variability in an operant task.* Unpublished manuscript.

Thelen, E., & Smith, L. B. (1998). Dynamic systems theories. In W. Damon (Series Ed.) & R. M. Lerner (Vol. Ed.), *Handbook of child psychology: Vol. 1. Theoretical models of human development* (5th ed.). New York: Wiley.

Thelen, E., & Ulrich, B. D. (1991). Hidden skills: A dynamic systems analysis of treadmill stepping during the first year. *Monographs of the Society for Research in Child Development, 56* (1, Serial No. 223).

Turiel, E., & Davidson, P. (1986). Heterogeneity, inconsistency, and asynchrony in the development of cognitive structures. In I. Levin (Ed.), *Stage and structure: Reopening the debate.* Norwood, NJ: Ablex.

Tversky, B., & Hemenway, D. (1984). Objects, parts, and categories. *Journal of Experimental Psychology: General, 113,* 169–193.

Visalberghi, E., & Limongelli, L. (1994). Lack of comprehension of cause-effect relations in tool-using capuchin monkeys (*cebus apella*). *Journal of Comparative Psychology, 108,* 15–22.

Wellman, H. M. (1990). *The child's theory of mind.* Cambridge, MA: MIT Press.

Wellman, H. M., & Gelman, S. A. (1998). Knowledge acquisition in foundational domains. In W. Damon (Series Ed.) & D. Kuhn & R. S. Siegler (Vol. Eds.), *Handbook of child psychology: Vol. 2. Cognition, perception & language* (5th ed.). New York: Wiley.

Wertsch, J. V., & Hickmann, M. (1987). Problem solving in social interaction: A microgenetic analysis. In M. Hickmann (Ed.), *Social and functional approaches to language and thought.* San Diego, CA: Academic Press.

Willatts, P. (1984). The Stage IV infant's solution of problems requiring the use of supports. *Infant Behavior and Development, 7,* 125–134.

Willatts, P. (1990). Development of problem solving strategies in infancy. In D. F. Bjorklund (Ed.), *Children's strategies.* Hillsdale, NJ: Erlbaum.

Willatts, P. (1998, April). *Development of means-end planning in the second year of life.* Paper presented at the biennial meeting of the International Society on Infant Studies, Atlanta, Georgia.

Willatts, P., & Rosie, K. (1989, April). *Planning by 12-month-old infants.* Paper presented at the biennial meeting of the Society for Research in Child Development, Kansas City, MO.

Willett, J. B. (1997). Measuring change: What individual growth modeling buys you. In E. Amsel & K. A. Renninger (Eds.), *Change and development: Issues of theory, method, and application.* Mahwah, NJ: Erlbaum.

Wood, D. J. (1989). Social interaction as tutoring. In M. H. Bornstein & J. S. Bruner (Eds.), *Interaction in human development.* Hillsdale, NJ: Erlbaum.

Wynn, K. (1998). Numerical competence in infants. In C. Donlan (Ed.), *The development of mathematical skills: Studies in developmental psychology.* Hove, East Sussex, England: Psychology Press.

Yarrow, M. R., Scott, P. M., & Waxler, C. Z. (1973). Learning concern for others. *Developmental Psychology, 8,* 240–260.

ACKNOWLEDGMENTS

This work was supported by grants from NICHD (HD 19011 and HD 35862) and by an NIH Post-Doctoral Fellowship (MH 19102). We thank Hee Hua, Nematullah Karimi, Denise Saenz, and Alice Siegler for data collection and transcription. Thanks also to the children and parents for their participation and cooperation. We are also grateful to Rachel K. Clifton, Judy DeLoache, and two anonymous reviewers for their thoughtful and helpful comments on an earlier version of this *Monograph*. Portions of the data were presented at the 11th Biennial International Conference on Infant Studies, Atlanta, Georgia, April 1998, and at the Biennial Meeting of the Society for Research in Child Development, Albuquerque, New Mexico, April 1999.

COMMENTARY

A KEY BRIDGE TO UNDERSTANDING THE DEVELOPMENT OF THINKING AND PROBLEM SOLVING

Marvin W. Daehler

A major difficulty for anyone attempting to write a commentary on this *Monograph* is selecting only a few of its many significant points to single out as the more noteworthy contributions. This work is filled with ample illustrations of informative, thought-provoking advances bearing on theory and methodology; as a consequence, it offers many insights into our understanding of toddlers and their early problem-solving capacities. The application of overlapping waves theory, and the detailed observations of performance over multiple tasks on which it hinges, seems like such an obvious way to explore cognitive development in 2-year-olds that the reader will surely ponder why it has taken so long to put the theory and method to the test.

Fortunately, Chen and Siegler help to ease our dismay over failing to recognize the enormous potential of a microgenetic analysis of toddler problem solving. They point out the problem of different agendas as well as different methods and measures often used to evaluate infant and toddler cognition compared to the cognitive development of older children. Questions directed at *when* capacities emerge have dominated the infant literature, whereas a focus on *how* various competencies are established has become an increasingly pointed concern in research with older children.

Yet it would be misleading to exaggerate the emphasis on the "when" question among infant researchers. The polemics surrounding the "how" question seem to occur on a different plane. The debate over how cognitive development proceeds during the first months and years of life typically has been framed within the controversy of nativism versus empiricism (cf., Haith, 1998; Haith & Benson, 1998; Spelke, 1998), an issue

97

that loses much of its potential interpretive appeal as examination of cognitive development shifts to older children. Given the difficulty of resolving the role of inborn mechanisms versus acquired factors with respect to cognition in infancy, we can be virtually assured that it will be an even more arduous task, and probably considerably less productive, for understanding later development. Wisely, investigators have steered away by focusing instead on the various component processes that underlie thinking and problem solving in older children. To our good fortune, Chen and Siegler have now effectively extended this approach to include toddlers.

The Power of Observation and the Persuasion of Hints

In applying overlapping waves theory and the microgenetic approach, Chen and Siegler have identified a number of component processes characterizing strategic behavior. The results provide insights relevant to many of these processes. Among them is the question of how new strategies are acquired. Certainly one of the more remarkable findings among the many reported in this work is just how essential it was for toddlers to observe a tool's use or receive a hint to initiate a tool selection strategy for successful performance on the task. Children in the control condition, left to their own devices, rarely engaged in a tool selection strategy, and as a consequence seldom succeeded in retrieving the toy. Indeed, there was little evidence that children, some approaching 3 years of age, were making any progress in implementing the tool selection strategy over the 15 trials of the task.

This finding is reminiscent of the results of another recently published microgenetic study of problem solving, involving 5- to 9-year-olds and a very different kind of problem (Thornton, 1999). The task was to create a bridge crossing over an imaginary "river." To do so, children had to use wooden blocks of the kind commonly found in various preschools. No single block was long enough, however, to span the river by itself. A successful solution required children to join two blocks (or possibly more) to cross the river. An additional constraint was that no block could be placed in the middle of the river to serve as a stanchion to support the juncture formed by the separate blocks. Thus, the weight of the blocks projecting over the river needed to be offset in some manner, for example, by assembling a tower of blocks atop the ends extending onto the river bank to act as a counterweight.

Needless to say, this was not an easy task to complete, even for the 7- and 9-year-olds. But consider the plight of 5-year-olds, who rarely were able to derive a solution. One 5-year-old did produce a correct solution right away. More interesting, only one of nine 5-year-olds *not* immediately successful came up with an acceptable resolution to the problem within the approximately 25 min permitted to work on the task. This child literally stumbled on the solution strategy while pressing her hands, and eventually other blocks she held in her hands, on opposite ends of the two spans to keep them joined and suspended above the river. In her analyses of these results, Thornton (1999) emphasized that constraints established within the problem itself permitted this child to arrive at the principle of counterbalance and led to her achieving the goal of the task, a reasonable explanation for that child's success. To repeat, however, only one of the nine 5-year-olds who spent any time working with these materials was able to come up with a solution strategy. In fact, one of the 5-year-olds devoted the entire 25-min period searching throughout the room for a single block of sufficient length to span the river!

Thornton's results, along with those observed in the Chen and Siegler control group, dramatically bring home the point that children, and very likely adults as well, are not always very good at inventing or detecting new strategies for solving problems when left to their own brute cognitive processing devices. Researchers have witnessed this difficulty elsewhere. For example, one of the most powerful influences on successful transfer involving analogical reasoning for both children and adults is that of noticing the relevant solution principle; hints are among the most effective ways of encouraging this process (Brown & Campione, 1984; Gick & Holyoak, 1980, 1983; Weisberg, DiCamillo, & Phillips, 1978). At every age we often seem to need assistance in coming up with new strategies just as it appeared to be very important for the toddlers in order for them to be successful.

Although Thornton did not provide a helping hand to the 5-year-olds in her study, the experience of watching as one of them searched for a block of sufficient length for the entire 25 min surely must have been a painful one. In fact, researchers often comment on how difficult it is for parents as well to avoid helping their children when attempting to solve a problem in an experimental setting. Perhaps that says something about their parenting concerns more broadly. It also has implications relevant to the enormous value of modeling and hints as resources for cognitive processing and for the development of learning more generally. Chen and Siegler present a helpful discussion about modeling and hints as factors for initiating cognitive change. They also comment on the rise and fall of learning as a central topic of study in psychology. Perhaps the two phenomena are more closely coupled than many investigators concerned with cognition are comfortable to admit. Researchers have traditionally focused on learning in very limited contexts. As psychologists simplified and sanitized experimental settings, procedures, and materials in order to test the basic processes underlying learning, they may well have removed some of the most powerful means by which cognitive development is promoted. That is, the richer context may provide the best opportunity to observe and become informed about becoming a better thinker and problem solver.

This is certainly not a revolutionary idea. Brown et al. (1983) emphasized that cognitive activity very often proceeds in the context of others rather than in isolation. For dialecticians, the matter of dialogue is pivotal to development (Vygotsky, 1978), and those who have built upon this theoretical tradition, along with many other psychologists, have expanded upon the central role that both verbal and nonverbal interactions play in cognitive development (Rogoff, 1990, 1998; Wood, 1989; Wood, Bruner, & Ross, 1976). But as Rogoff (1998) pointed out in a recent review of studies concerned with cognition as a collaborative process, the notion still seems to be novel for many researchers. Perhaps the findings presented here will help to convince us that modeling, hints, and other informational contexts can provide an integral link to establishing new strategies. A major issue then becomes one of determining what kinds of instruction the toddler can most effectively assimilate into his or her understanding of the problem to be solved.

Still Other Divides to Conquer?

The use of the microgenetic approach as a means of crossing the great divide has paid off handsomely in helping to appreciate the strategic behavior of toddlers. But are there other divides yet to cross? Another interesting finding in the present study was that the older and younger toddlers differed in the degree to which they benefited from the experimenter's verbal hints to use a tool. This age difference was not evident when children could observe the experimenter select a tool to obtain the toy. Both experimental procedures appeared equally effective for the older children but not for the younger children, as a smaller proportion of the younger children seemed to respond to the verbal hint. Chen and Siegler suggest that the modeling of tool selection and its use offered more concrete information than did the verbal hint. That is a reasonable explanation for the age and condition differences, but the finding also raises other questions. For example, what might the results have looked like for even younger children than those tested in this study? Based on the research on imitation with 12- to 18-month-olds (e.g., Barr & Hayne, 1999; Meltzoff & Moore, 1999), perhaps they, too, would have had some success, at least with respect to the modeling condition. Would the verbal hints, however, have promoted a tool selection strategy at this earlier age? Perhaps not, because of limits in verbal comprehension. More important, the difference reported in this *Monograph* between performance in the modeling and verbal hint conditions further opens the door to another persistent problem: how language affects our thinking and problem solving.

The relevance of the potential great divide associated with language's influence on thought comes from one other bit of information. At several places in this *Monograph*, Chen and Siegler note that the microgenetic approach for studying toddlers mirrored the way it has been carried out with older children—*with one exception.* That exception was the inability to exploit verbal reports from toddlers as a means of revealing their strategy use. This methodological limitation does not detract from the findings in the *Monograph.* The lack of access to verbal resources, however, along with the differences reported for the effectiveness of certain kinds of assistance, highlights the reality that older children are able to both interpret and represent strategies in linguistic form, whereas infants are unable to do so (or do so much less effectively). This divide still has to be crossed. Here again we are confronted with an issue that has plagued developmental psychology from its beginning, but one that continues unresolved. What exactly is the nature of the representations available to the infant and toddler that underlie their cognition, or in this particular case, strategic behavior? And is it possible that developmental changes with respect to these, for example, the appearance of propositional or linguistically based representations, have a substantial bearing on both children's conceptual understanding and the particular components of their strategic activity such as acquiring, mapping, or effectively executing strategy choices? The results of the present study are comforting in suggesting that a microgenetic analysis yields extremely valuable information about strategic development despite the lack of availability of verbal reports. The jury remains out, however, on whether the development of symbolic representational systems has important consequences for the various component processes underlying problem solving. And even if the nature of the available representations has little bearing on the fundamental components of strategic learning, it surely has implications for the kinds of context in which their acquisition is fostered. In fact, it is conceivable that for older children certain kinds of learning may proceed more effectively as a result of being told, rather than observing, what to do.

Biases and Knowledge

One of the most exciting aspects of the microgenetic approach is how much information it provides about mapping, strengthening, refining, and executing strategies in addition to their acquisition. Chen and Siegler were able to offer insights for each of these learning components as a result of the innovative design of their study. Various types of stimulus or response biases, often a part of the behavioral repertoire of very young children, apparently were not seen with sufficient frequency to be considered among the "strategies." Because children in the control condition generally did not engage in tool selection, any bias, such as picking out a specific tool or a tool in a particular location in the array, would not have been easy to measure. Furthermore, in the experimental conditions, perhaps the modeling or hint was sufficiently powerful to override possible position or other response tendencies so that refinement of the correct tool selection strategy did not compete with such biases. Position biases and perseverative response have been reported most frequently in somewhat different kinds of problems, for example, in classic discrimination tasks or where retrieval of hidden objects is a central aspect of the situation (e.g., DeLoache, 1999; O'Sullivan, Mitchell, & Daehler, 1999; Stevenson, 1972; Zelazo, Reznick, & Spinazzola, 1998). The absence of response biases and stimulus preferences in the tool-use problem helped to make the analysis of tool selection strategies far more manageable.

In reporting the results concerned with the refinement of strategy choices, Chen and Siegler note that at least some children entered the problem-solving task with an understanding of the tool-use strategy. For example, on the first three trials of the problem, before they were given encouragement to select a tool, children used one or more tools on about 20% of the trials. On these trials children also were more likely to choose the longer tool, and, among the longer ones, they were more likely to use the tool with a head than would be expected by chance. But we need to be cautious in making inferences about the type of knowledge children possess about the tools at the beginning of the task. For example, some toddlers, as Chen and Siegler conclude, may realize that the length of the tool is the relevant aspect in determining which one should be chosen. It also is possible, however, that the typically closer proximity of the endpoints of the longer tools in relation to the toy made them better candidates than the shorter tools for trying to make contact with the toy. Alternative interpretations for why children chose tools with heads more frequently than tools without heads are less easy to generate. But until a simple preference test is carried out evaluating the extent to which children this age interact with a tool (in a context other than using it to retrieve a toy), we cannot eliminate other potential explanations for these choices as well.

These are relatively minor points. Perhaps the real power of the type of research described in this *Monograph* comes from the opportunities created to explore other questions about strategic behavior, problem solving, and transfer in very young children. Is the positioning of the tools a factor? For example, would children this age, as a consequence of particular kinds of instructions, generalize the tool selection strategy to arrays in which the tools are set out on a table to the side of the child rather than immediately in front and in the line of sight for reaching for the toy? How durable are the strategies once they are acquired? For example, if some type of intervening activity took place between the problems, would younger and older toddlers show the same levels of transfer and might instructional condition have a bearing on this as well? These are just a couple of the many possibilities for further exploring the path, rate, breadth, variability, and sources of cognitive change in toddlers. A major purpose of the present study was to begin the task of understanding these dimensions of change in the toddler years; the results have provided a superb foundation on which to continue to build this understanding.

Some Concluding Comments

Many other important findings could be highlighted. For example, boys displayed greater success than girls at retrieving the toy, probably because they also were more likely to use a tool strategy. Does this sex difference arise from the generally higher activity level typically ascribed to boys? Or perhaps from a greater orientation toward instrumentality or some other social or personality characteristic that differentiates the behaviors of boys and girls? Or are the sex differences somehow linked to the spatial aspects of this particular type of problem or a few of the basic components of strategic behavior? Sex differences have not always been found in other types of tasks involving tool use. For example, in a recent study in our laboratory 30-month-old girls, after observing a model, were as likely as boys to select the correct tool and imitate its appropriate action from among various tools associated with a child's workbench (Mac-Connell, 2000).

Noteworthy, too, is the chapter on individual differences in learning, an aspect of developmental research that all too rarely is included in studies of thinking and problem solving. As Chen and Siegler emphasize, the microgenetic approach is particularly useful in being able to provide such information. Especially informative here was the attempt to identify the influences of both distal (e.g., age, sex, and training condition) and proximal factors (the various components of learning taking place within the task) on the performance of a tool selection strategy.

My guess is that readers will find many other positive aspects pertaining to the theory, method, and findings reported in this *Monograph*. That is one of the primary reasons that this work will gain wide recognition. It reflects a pivotal approach to bridging the gap between infancy and older children and will help to reconcile the different vistas that seem so apparent when looking to either side of the great divide. Just as important, I suspect the route along which this work has traveled will be one many researchers will follow, and find extraordinarily valuable, in their efforts to integrate the very different perspectives that, from the present vantage point, seem to veil our understanding of how cognition in infants corresponds with cognition in older children.

References

Barr, R., & Hayne, H. (1999). Developmental changes in imitation from television during infancy. *Child Development, 70*, 1067–1081.

Brown, A. L., Bransford, J. D., Ferrara, R. A., & Campione, J. C. (1983). Learning, remembering, and understanding. In P. H. Mussen (Series Ed.) & J. H. Flavell & E. M. Markman (Vol. Eds.), *Handbook of child psychology: Vol. 3. Cognitive development* (4th ed.). New York: Wiley.

Brown, A. L., & Campione, J. C. (1984). Three faces of transfer: Implications for early competence, individual differences and instruction. In M. E. Lamb, A. L. Brown, & B. Rogoff (Eds.), *Advances in developmental psychology* (Vol. 3). Hillsdale, NJ: Erlbaum.

DeLoache, J. S. (1999, April). *Inhibitory control and symbol use.* Paper presented at the biennial meetings of the Society for Research in Child Development, Albuquerque, NM.

Gick, M. L., & Holyoak, K. J. (1980). Analogical problem solving. *Cognitive Psychology, 12*, 306–355.

Gick, M. L., & Holyoak, K. J. (1983). Schema induction and analogical transfer. *Cognitive Psychology, 15*, 1–38.

Haith, M. M. (1998). Who put the cog in infant cognition? Is rich interpretation too costly? *Infant Behavior and Development, 21*, 167–179.

Haith, M. M., & Benson, J. (1998). Infant cognition. In W. Damon (Series Ed.) & D. Kuhn & R. S. Siegler (Vol. Eds.), *Handbook of child psychology: Vol. 2. Cognition, perception, and language* (5th ed.). New York: Wiley.

MacConnell, A. (2000). *Symbolic functioning: Extending the dual representation issue beyond the classic model/room paradigm.* Unpublished master's thesis, University of Massachusetts, Amherst, MA.

Meltzoff, A. N., & Moore, M. K. (1999). Persons and representation: Why infant imitation is important for theories of human development. In J. Nadel & G. Butterworth (Eds.), *Imitation in infancy*. Cambridge, UK: Cambridge University Press.

O'Sullivan, L. P., Mitchell, L. L., & Daehler, M. W. (1999, October). *The role of perseverative errors in performance on scale model tasks.* Poster session presented at the first biennial meeting of the Cognitive Development Society, Chapel Hill, NC.

Rogoff, B. (1990). *Apprenticeship in thinking: Cognitive development in social context.* New York: Oxford University Press.

Rogoff, B. (1998). Cognition as a collaborative process. In W. Damon (Series Ed.) & D. Kuhn & R. S. Siegler (Vol. Eds.), *Handbook of child psychology: Vol. 2. Cognition, perception, and language* (5th ed.). New York: Wiley.

Siegler, R. S., & Jenkins, E. (1989). *How children discover new strategies.* Hillsdale, NJ: Erlbaum.

Spelke, E. (1998). Nativism, empiricism, and the origins of knowledge. *Infant Behavior and Development, 21*, 181–200.

Stevenson, H. W. (1972). *Children's learning.* New York: Appleton-Century-Crofts.

Thornton, S. (1999). Creating the conditions for cognitive change: The interaction between task structures and specific strategies. *Developmental Psychology,* **70**, 588–603.

Vygotsky, L. S. (1978). *Mind in society: The development of higher psychological processes.* Cambridge, MA: Harvard University Press.

Weisberg, R. W., DiCamillo, M., & Phillips, D. (1978). Transferring old associations to new problems: A non-automatic process. *Journal of Verbal Learning & Verbal Behavior,* **17**, 219–228.

Wood, D. J. (1989). Social interaction as tutoring. In M. H. Bornstein & J. S. Bruner (Eds.), *Interaction in human development.* Hillsdale, NJ: Erlbaum.

Wood, D. J., Bruner, J. S., & Ross, G. (1976). The role of tutoring in problem-solving. *Journal of Child Psychology and Psychiatry,* **17**, 89–100.

Zelazo, P. D., Reznick, J. S., & Spinazzola, J. (1998). Representational flexibility and response control in a multistep multilocation search task. *Developmental Psychology,* **34**, 203–214.

CONTRIBUTORS

Zhe Chen (Ph.D. 1991, University of Massachusetts, Amherst) is an assistant professor in the department of Human and Community Development at the University of California, Davis. His research focuses on the mechanisms involved in children's thinking and learning processes. Current research interests include three interrelated lines of inquiry: analogical problem solving; scientific reasoning; and microgenetic analyses of strategy acquisition.

Robert S. Siegler (Ph.D. 1974, State University of New York at Stony Brook) is Teresa Heinz Professor of Cognitive Psychology at Carnegie Mellon University. Much of his recent research focuses on how children choose among existing strategies and how they discover new strategies. He is author of *Emerging Minds* (1996) and *Children's Thinking* (1998).

Marvin W. Daehler (Ph.D. 1968, University of Minnesota) is professor of psychology and the graduate program director at the University of Massachusetts. His recent research interests include the development of analogical reasoning, the emergence of symbolic capacities in very young children, and transfer in problem solving.

STATEMENT OF EDITORIAL POLICY

The Monographs series is devoted to publishing developmental research that generates authoritative new findings and uses these to foster fresh, better integrated, or more coherent perspectives on major developmental issues, problems, and controversies. The significance of the work in extending developmental theory and contributing definitive empirical information in support of the conceptual advance, is the most critical editorial consideration. Along with advancing knowledge on specialized topics, the series aims to enhance cross-fertilization among developmental disciplines and developmental sub fields. Therefore, clarity of the links between the specific issues under study and questions relating to general developmental processes is important. These links, as well as the manuscript as a whole, must be as clear to the general reader as to the specialist. The selection of manuscripts for editorial consideration, and the shaping of manuscripts through reviews-and-revisions, are processes dedicated to actualizing these ideals as closely as possible.

Typically Monographs entail programmatic large-scale investigations; sets of programmatic interlocking studies; or—in some cases—smaller studies with highly definitive and theoretically significant empirical findings. Multiauthored sets of independent studies that center on the same underlying question can also be appropriate; a critical requirement here is that all authors address common issues and that the contribution arising from the set as a whole be unique, substantial, and well integrated. In essence, irrespective of how it may be framed, any work that is judged to significantly extend developmental thinking will be taken under editorial consideration.

To be considered, submissions should meet the editorial goals of Monographs and should be no briefer than a minimum of 80 pages (including references and tables). There is an upper limit of 150–175 pages. Only in exceptional circumstances will this upper limit be modified. (please submit four copies). Because a Monograph is inevitable lengthy and usually substantively complex, it is particularly important that the text be well organized and written in clear, precise, and literate English. Note, however, that authors from non-English speaking countries should not be put off by this stricture. In accordance with the general aims of SRCD, this series is actively interested in promoting international exchange of developmental research. Neither membership in the Society nor affiliation with the academic discipline of psychology are relevant in considering a *Monographs* submission.

The corresponding author for any manuscript must, in the submission letter, warrant that all coauthors are in agreement with the content of the manuscript. The corresponding author also is responsible for informing all coauthors, in a timely manner, of manuscript submission, editorial decisions, reviews received, and any revisions recommended. Before publication, the corresponding author also must warrant in the submission letter that the study has been conducted according to the ethical guidelines of the Society for Research in Child Development.

Willis F. Overton, Editor
Temple University-Psychology
1701 North 13th St, Rm 567
Philadelphia, PA 19122-6085

Editorial Office
Danielle L. Horvath, Editorial Assistant
Tel: +1 215 204 7718
Email: monosrcd@blue.vm.temple.edu